The Essence of International Money

2nd Edition

THE ESSENCE OF MANAGEMENT SERIES

PUBLISHED TITLES

The Essence of International Money

2nd Edition

ADRIAN BUCKLEY
Cranfield School of Management

Prentice Hall

London New York Toronto Sydney Tokyo Singapore
Madrid Mexico City Munich

First published 1990
This edition published 1996 by
Prentice Hall International (UK) Limited
Campus 400, Maylands Avenue
Hemel Hempstead
Hertfordshire, HP2 7EZ
A division of
Simon & Schuster International Group

Typeset in 10/12pt Palatino
by Keyset Composition, Colchester, Essex

Printed and bound in Great Britain by
Redwood Books Limited, Trowbridge, Wiltshire

Library of Congress Cataloging-in-Publication Data

Available from the publisher

British Library Cataloguing in Publication Data

A catalogue record for this book is available from
the British Library

ISBN 0-13-356494-0

---

1 2 3 4 5   00 99 98 97 96

Contents

Preface

The growth of international business and deregulation of financial markets has changed the face of financial management in the last couple of decades. Twenty-five years ago managers could be relatively complacent about foreign exchange risk; after all we were operating in a world of fixed exchange rates with widespread exchange controls – at least in most of Europe. The move towards floating exchange rates and the dismantling of exchange controls in Britain and many other countries put an end to this complacency. Understanding what impelled international financial markets became imperative, although it is doubtful whether, even now, British managers know as much as they should about foreign exchange markets and their implications. To some extent – but by no means in total – Britain's loss of market share in world trade might be attributed to such ignorance.

Despite the growth in international business over the recent past, good basic texts on international money are conspicuous by their absence from managers' bookshelves. True, there is a pile of high-priced, complex texts in the subject area, but the basic book that provides a foundation for non-financial managers and for students of international business is not around. It is this gap in the market that is addressed by this modestly priced text. If the author succeeds, the reader will obtain a foundation in the understanding of foreign exchange markets, their workings, their value, uses and their implications. And if this objective is met then readers may wish to move on to more advanced texts in the subject area.

My intent, then, is truly practical. It is that this text should improve performance and awareness by introducing readers with no prior knowledge of international financial management (but with a basic understanding of domestic finance) to the essence of international money.

I am most grateful to Liz Tribe who cheerfully typed the manuscript and generally acted as manager in putting the book into a format fit for publication. Having said this, responsibility for errors remains my own.

Adrian Buckley

Introduction

Twenty years ago the majority of company executives did not have to understand what impelled exchange rates to move or how to avoid foreign exchange risk. Decisions to move away from the fixed exchange rate system and to disband exchange controls were important factors in changing all that. Managers had to start to learn new tricks in the 1970s and 1980s. Those who were slow to learn made mistakes. They failed to cover Deutsche Mark payables as sterling declined precipitously; they borrowed in Swiss francs because the interest cost was low; they failed to realize the opportunities created by the demise of exchange controls; they were unaware of the benefits to accrue from currency options, and so on. Unfortunately, even now there is too much ignorance about international financial management. This text aims to combat perceived gaps in managers' knowledge in a readable, comprehensible and logical way. In so doing, the intent is to avoid mathematics but a small amount inevitably has to occur. But not too much, I trust.

Financial management is concerned with the costs of financing sources and the payoffs from investment. In the domestic arena, movements in exchange rates are substantially ignored; but when we move outside of the purely domestic field, there is no way that we can analyse international financing and investment opportunities without an understanding of the impact of foreign exchange rates upon the basic model of financial management. We are still concerned with raising funds at minimum cost, but there are clearly complications if a British-based or a French company is raising funds by way of a Swiss franc borrowing. We are still concerned with investment opportunities chosen to create maximum shareholder value, but what if the income and cash flow of our British-based or French company's investments arise from Switzerland in Swiss francs? Or from

Mexico in pesos? And what if exchange controls place barriers on remittances of some proportion of profit?

Obviously international financial management possesses a dimension that makes it far more complicated than its domestic counterpart. Indeed we make no bones about it: multinational finance is a complex area of study. It has been sired by the internationalization of business. If money is the language of business, foreign exchange is the language of international business.

We are therefore concerned in the early chapters of this book with foreign exchange markets throughout the world and with the pressures that impel exchange rates to move upwards and downwards. In later chapters, we look at topics like foreign currency exposure and how to avoid it, international investment appraisal, multinational financing and so on.

The objective of this text is to provide a general, basic book which meets the needs of managers and students coming to the foreign exchange market for the first time. There is a bibliography at the end of the book which has been prepared to guide the reader's next steps in multinational finance should he or she wish to move onwards. But this book is unashamedly a general text – which is what the Essence series is all about.

1

What is international money all about?

With any topic, there are certain factors which set the scene and are essential to an understanding of the subject. This is as true of international money as it is of beekeeping. In this first chapter we present some of these key factors about foreign exchange markets and the Eurocurrency markets – the pillars of international money. The reality of foreign exchange is, however, that it is such a dynamic subject that data on market sizes presented here will, no doubt, be overtaken by events before this book is published.

The foreign exchange markets

For the majority of foreign exchange markets, there are no individual, physical marketplaces. The market is made up of banks and dealers carrying out transactions via telephone, computer, telex and other similar devices.

The total world foreign exchange market is the largest of all markets in the world. It has been estimated that foreign exchange deals, worldwide, averaged $1300 billion per day in 1995 – a doubling of the figure three years earlier. This market size is two hundred times that of the New York Stock Exchange. The market is a twenty-four-hour market which moves from one centre to another – from Tokyo to Hong Kong to Singapore to Kuwait to London to New York to San Francisco to Sydney and then back to Tokyo – as the sun appears to move round the world. Figure 1.1 summarizes the overlap.

About 95 per cent of all foreign exchange transactions involve banks on both sides of the deal. This high percentage is reflected by banks taking and unravelling positions in currencies in order to trade for profit and to

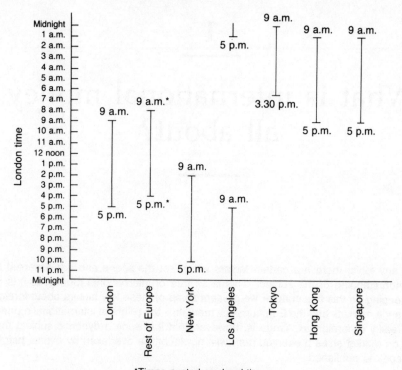

*Times quoted are local time.

Figure 1.1 Time overlap of world foreign exchange markets.

offset imbalances created by their purchases and sales with customers. Some 95 per cent of all trades involve the US dollar. If a French importer wishes to pay a British exporter, the bank will quote a sterling/franc rate based upon the franc/dollar rate and the dollar/sterling rate.

Nowadays, trade accounts for only a small proportion of all foreign exchange deals, maybe only 1 to 2 per cent of total transactions. The lion's share is made up of capital movements from one centre to another and the taking of positions by bankers in different currencies.

There is a spot market in which deals are arranged for immediate delivery (technically, a spot deal has delivery two working days after the spot transaction) and there is a forward market in which purchase or sale is arranged today at an agreed rate but with delivery some time in the future. Forward markets do not exist for all currencies, for example there is no forward market for the Argentine peso. But, for the currencies of major western economies, forward markets can go out to ten years; for others it is only in existence for up to six months or a year. The term deep market is used to refer to those currencies which are widely dealt, for example dollars, sterling, Deutsche Marks, etc. At the opposite end of the spectrum, the terms shallow or thin market are applied synonymously to currencies which are traded only occasionally.

London is the largest foreign exchange centre, followed by New York and then Tokyo. London's average daily turnover is around $464bn; the next two centres' averages amount to $244bn and $161bn, respectively. Half of London's turnover is accounted for by spot transactions and almost 40 per cent involves forward deals maturing within one month.

The foreign exchange market is the cheapest market in the world in which to deal. If one were to start with US$1m and switch this into Deutsche Marks and then immediately reverse the transaction so that one returned to US dollars, the proceeds would be less than US$1m by approximately twice the bid/offer spread (the rate for selling and the rate for buying) for Deutsche Marks against US dollars (after all, two deals have been done). But assuming exchange rates had not moved, the total amount by which one would be out of pocket would be only $300 or so. For major currencies, the large banks act as market makers. This means that they hold stocks of foreign currencies and are prepared to deal in large amounts at stated prices. In other currencies, banks may operate as brokers thereby avoiding the risk of price movements.

Foreign exchange dealers can make or lose a lot of money for the banks that employ them. They can make a million dollars a day for the bank, but they can also lose that sum. Their salaries and bonuses are high: some make $500,000 per annum. But their business life is strenuous. Watching currency movements for ten hours a day in the bank (and taking a Reuters foreign exchange rate screen home) and dealing on the finest margins all take their toll. Dealers on banks' foreign exchange desks seem to be aged between twenty and just over thirty. Perhaps beyond thirty, reflexes are slower. Perhaps the adrenalin flows more slowly. Or maybe dealers have made so much money already that motivation is not quite what it used to be and dealers move onto a less frenetic life style.

Eurocurrency markets

With a few minor exceptions, the definition of a Eurodollar is a dollar deposited in a bank outside of the USA. A Eurodeutsche Mark is a Deutsche Mark deposited in a bank outside Germany. A Eurosterling deposit is created by depositing British pounds in a bank account outside of the UK. The term Eurocurrency is used to embrace all forms of Euro-deposits. But beware. When people talk about the Eurodollar market a certain amount of caution is called for. This is because the term Eurodollars is sometimes used as a generic term for all Eurocurrency deposits.

Eurocurrency markets exist outside of the borders of the country of the underlying currency concerned. As such, they escape controls which may be imposed on domestic currency markets. Indeed, they escape controls altogether. Markets for lending and borrowing in Eurocurrencies operate in the world of classical economies – a world without a regulating authority, a world without controls. In this respect, a contrast must be drawn with domestic currency and domestic money markets.

The domestic central bank is usually the institution through which the home government intervenes in domestic interest rate markets and currency markets. In Eurocurrency and Euro-interest rate markets there is no intervention by a central bank for Euromarkets because there is no central bank for Euromarkets.

In domestic interest rate markets governments have, at various points in the past, fixed maximum interest rates payable by commercial banks to depositors. In domestic banking markets, governments frequently specify that banks must deposit some proportion of their own lendings to clients or deposits received from customers with the local central bank at rates substantially below market rates – so-called reserve asset requirements.

The effect of the former control was that it forced depositors to seek market rates by placing their monies in non-regulated markets, such as Euromarkets. Via this kind of mechanism, investors have been able to access higher deposits in Euromarkets than they have in domestic markets.

The impact of the latter control, exercised through reserve asset requirements, has a similar distorting effect. With reserve requirements, a commercial bank aiming for a return of, say, 15 per cent per annum on its total loan portfolio would have to charge borrowers above this rate in order to compensate for the placing of monies with the central bank at a submarket rate. By contrast, in the Euromarkets the commercial bank would lend at 15 per cent per annum to earn an overall return of 15 per cent since no requirements for below market rate depositing exist. All other things being equal, borrowers are able to access Euromarkets more cheaply than their domestic counterpart.

It is interesting to note that the effect of the domestic regulations referred to in the foregoing paragraph means that both lenders and borrowers may get a better deal in the Euromarkets than in the domestic markets. Hardly surprising, then, that Euromarkets offer a vast reservoir of lending and borrowing potential for companies, governments, quasi-government organizations, high net worth individuals and so on. It is also worth noting that, in the absence of exchange controls, Euromarkets and domestic markets should not get much out of line since it is always possible for an operator (whether an individual, or a company or a bank) to borrow in the Euromarket and invest in the domestic market. The possibility of arbitrage of this kind should keep rates fairly close.

The advantages referred to above are based upon regulation of domestic financial markets as opposed to non-regulation of Euromarkets. To some extent, deregulation of domestic markets is putting these two marketplaces onto the same footing. The Euromarkets have, nonetheless, developed a momentum of their own and they have experienced no problem in terms of maintaining their attractiveness to investors and borrowers alike – even though domestic markets are frequently quite competitive.

The key significance of Euromarkets in much of our analysis of international finance is that they represent unregulated (or free) markets in which to place money or to borrow. In other words, these markets demonstrate the unfettered interaction of demand and supply in arriving at the price of money.

The genesis of the Eurocurrency markets in the 1950s occurred because Soviet government agencies wanted to maintain currency deposits in dollars. This was because the dollar was the most acceptable currency for financing their international transactions. They were reluctant to hold their dollars in deposits in New York since the threat existed that the US authorities might freeze these deposits. So the dollars held by the USSR moved to London as the Soviets believed that the political risk of London dollar deposits was lower than in New York. And the banks in which these offshore dollars were deposited on-lent thus giving birth to the Eurocurrency market.

While the Soviets may have been the cause of the rapid growth of offshore deposits during the 1950s, the really big take-off in the 1960s reflected other factors. The foremost of these was the increasing differential between Eurodollar and domestic interest rates, which made it increasingly profitable to escape national regulations in the USA. On top of this, growth was fuelled by the increasing size of the multinational firm and the great competitive expansion of banks. The Eurocurrency markets were on the move, and they have not stopped advancing.

2

The essence of currency calculations

Multinational financing management involves manipulation with more than one currency. Its understanding necessarily involves confronting such questions as how foreign exchange markets work, what makes exchange rates move and how protection can be bought to avoid currency risk. Making sense of the complexities of international finance has no magic answer – but this chapter presents the single most important theorem of foreign exchange. Without understanding it, the serious student will always flounder in the dark when confronted with exchange rates and interest rates. But if it is understood, a light appears at the end of the tunnel. The key to understanding the mysteries of this fascinating facet of finance is at hand. The secret concerns the relationship between interest rates, inflation rates, spot and forward exchange rates.

Foreign exchange markets

An American company importing goods from West Germany with their price denominated in Deutsche Marks may buy marks in order to pay for the goods. An American company exporting goods to Germany, again with the price denominated in Marks, receives Deutsche Marks which it may then sell in exchange for dollars. The currency aspects of these transactions involve use of the foreign exchange markets.

In most centres, the foreign exchange market has no central, physical marketplace. Business is conducted by telephone or telex. The main dealers are commercial banks and central banks. Most companies wishing to buy or sell currency usually do so through a commercial bank.

In the UK, exchange rates are quoted in terms of the number of units of foreign currency bought for one unit of home currency, that is £1. This method of quotation is termed the indirect quote. By contrast, exchange rates throughout continental Europe are quoted in terms of the number of units of home currency, that is the number of Deutsche Marks, French francs or whatever, necessary to buy one unit of foreign currency. This is the direct quotation method. In the USA, the convention is to use the direct quote when dealing internally with residents of the USA and the indirect quote when dealing with foreigners. The exception to this latter rule is that the direct quote is used when dealing with British-based banks or UK businesses. This practice means that New York uses the same figure when talking to foreign dealers as such foreign dealers use for their own transactions and quotations. A quote of $0.7271 per DM in New York means that each Deutsche Mark costs $0.7271. In other words, to put it in indirect terms, there are DM1.3753 to the dollar given by:

$$\frac{1}{0.7271}$$

On the face of it, buying or selling a currency at the spot rate of exchange implies immediate delivery and payment. The practice of the foreign exchange market is for delivery to be at two working days after the deal – but this applies only to spot transactions.

There is also the forward market where deals are for future delivery – usually one, three, six or twelve months' time, although other durations can be dealt. The forward market enables companies and others to insure themselves against foreign exchange losses (or, of course, to speculate on future movements to exchange rates). If you are going to need DM100,000 in six months' time, you can enter into a six-month forward contract. The forward rate on this contract is the price agreed now to be paid in six months when the DM100,000 are delivered.

If the six-month forward rate for the Deutsche Mark against the dollar is quoted at $0.7331 per DM as opposed to a spot price of $0.7271, the implication is that you pay more dollars if you buy forward than if you buy Deutsche Marks spot. In this case the dollar is said to trade at a forward discount on the Deutsche Mark. Put another way, the Deutsche Mark trades at a forward premium on the dollar. Expressed as an annual rate, the forward premium is:

$$\frac{(0.7331 - 0.7271)}{0.7271} \times \frac{12 \text{ months}}{6 \text{ months}} \times 100 = 1.65\% \text{ p.a.}$$

Assuming that forward markets and interest rates are in equilibrium, the currency of the country with the higher interest rate is said to be at a discount on the other currency. At the same time, looking at things from the opposite side of the fence, the currency of the country with lower interest rates will be at a premium on the other currency.

	s_0	= spot rate now
£/\$ exchange rates	f_0	= forward rate now
	$^*s_t$	= expected spot rate at time t
Interest rates per annum	i_s	= Eurodollar interest rate
	$i_£$	= Eurosterling interest rate
	p_s	= US general price level now
Inflation rates per annum	$p_£$	= UK general price level now
	$^*p_s$	= expected US inflation rate
	$^*p_£$	= expected UK inflation rate

Figure 2.1 Foreign exchange notation to be used.

Inflation, interest and exchange rates

In the absence of barriers to international capital mobility, there is a relationship between spot exchange rates, forward rates, interest rates and inflation rates. Many national governments attempt to restrict the mobility of their citizens' money; they erect exchange controls and they seek to regulate domestic interest rate markets. But money is internationally mobile in the Eurocurrency markets which are unfettered by government controls. Before considering the relationship between the four variables referred to, it will be helpful to set out the notation to be used. This appears in Figure 2.1.

It can be shown by deductive reasoning or by a mathematical approach that, if equilibrium holds, differences between forward and spot rates, differences in interest rates, expected differences in inflation rates and expected changes in spot rates are equal to one another. Figure 2.2 summarizes the relationship. A form of proof of the relationship is available in the appendix to Chapter 2 but this can be omitted without affecting basic understanding of the ideas developed in this text.

It must be stressed that the model in Figure 2.2 is an equilibrium model. In the real world, markets move towards equilibrium but rarely demonstrate total equilibrium at any particular point in time. So it should not be surprising if some of the arms of the four-way equivalence model do not hold in the real world of financial markets in the short term.

According to Figure 2.2, the relationship between the spot and the forward exchange rate is underpinned by interest rate differentials. Note, and this is most important, that we should be looking at free market interest rates, that is those quoted in the unfettered Eurocurrency markets; it is these that underpin the difference between spot and forward foreign

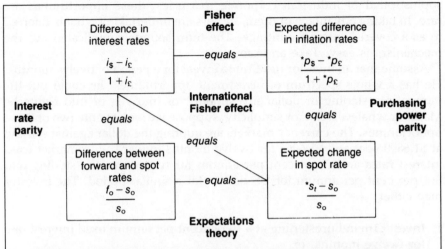

Figure 2.2 Four-way equivalence in the foreign exchange market.

Note: Using the notation as here, f_o, s_o and $^*s_t$ must all be stated in terms of the number of dollars to one pound sterling. Great care must be taken on this point whenever using the equations in the model. Should currencies other than dollars and sterling be under consideration, substitution in the model is a relatively simple process. To get approximate results, the number of months may be used. Thus a three-month forward premium or discount would have to be treated as:

$$\frac{f_o - s_o}{s_o} \times \frac{12}{3}$$

In practice, the actual number of days, rather than months, has to be used in calculations. A further slight modification is necessary because US dollar interest rates are quoted on a 360-day year basis whereas sterling rates are quoted on a 365-day basis.

Approximation
For quick, approximate calculations the four-way relationship may be written as:

$$i_\$ - i_£ = {}^*p_\$ - {}^*p_£ = \frac{f_o - s_o}{s_o} = \frac{{}^*s_t - s_o}{s_o}$$

This approximation becomes less accurate as higher inflation economies are dealt with.

exchange rates. This relationship is technically referred to as interest rate parity although it clearly involves exchange rates as well as interest rates. In Eurocurrency markets, interest rate parity is found to hold good virtually all of the time. That is not to say that bankers and dealers do not have opportunities to make profits from temporary disequilibria in interest rates and exchange rates; indeed, they make substantial profits from such sources. However, except at the level of bankers, dealers and the most sophisticated of industrial corporate treasuries, these opportunities are rare. In taking advantage of them, dealers are undertaking what is referred to as a covered interest arbitrage. The term sounds complicated but the mechanism is easy. Take an example.

Assume that an investor has £1m to invest for a period of twelve months. He has a whole spectrum of investment opportunities; he could put the money into sterling or dollar investments, or into yen or into Deutsche Marks or whatever. But for simplicity, suppose we look at only two of these opportunities. The currency markets are quoting the dollar against sterling at $1.6800 spot and $1.6066 for twelve months forward. Euromarket fixed interest rates are 13 per cent per annum for twelve months sterling and 8¹⁄₁₆ per cent per annum for US dollars for a similar period. The investor may either:

1. Invest £1m in Eurosterling at a 13 per cent per annum fixed interest rate for twelve months; or
2. Convert £1m into US dollars at $1.6800; invest the proceeds in the Eurodollar interest market at an 8¹⁄₁₆ per cent per annum fixed interest rate for one year and sell the pre-calculated proceeds forward twelve months at a rate of $1.6066.

What are the expected proceeds? Obviously the sterling investment yields £1,130,000 at the end of twelve months. The dollar investment yields, to all intents and purposes, the same amount. The proceeds from the spot transaction are $1,680,000. Investing at 8¹⁄₁₆ per cent per annum, the proceeds in twelve months' time will total $1,815,450 and selling this forward at $1.6066 yields £1,129,995. This is, more or less, the same outturn as from the sterling investment opportunity. This is what one might expect: after all, each investment opportunity is of equal risk (the investor carries the credit risk associated with the bank with whom he invests, but if he invests with the same Eurobank then the credit risk associated with each opportunity is equal), and investments of equal risk should, according to financial theory, promise equal returns.

Were this not the case, arbitrageurs in the foreign exchange and interest rate markets would borrow currency in one centre, swap it to the other, invest there and sell the proceeds forward. Such proceeds would, if equilibrium did not hold, exceed the amount repayable in terms of the borrowing plus accrued interest and thereby yield a virtually riskless profit to the operator. This mechanism is the covered interest arbitrage referred to earlier. The actions of dealers ensure that profitable opportunities of this kind do not last for more than fleeting instants. Exploitation of these brief opportunities creates movements in spot and forward exchange rates and in interest rates, and such movements ensure that the tendency in the currency and interest rate markets is towards equilibrium.

Covered interest arbitrage involves borrowing in centre A for a specified period at a fixed interest rate and shipping and proceeds borrowed to centre B. The sum shipped is deposited there for the same period as the borrowing in centre A, again at a fixed interest rate. The total proceeds of investment in centre B that will accrue at the end of the investment period can be calculated, since the interest rate is fixed. Such proceeds are sold via the forward market for the period of the borrowing and lending, and the sum received in centre A from this forward transaction will more than repay the borrowing in centre A plus accrued interest. This profit is said to be a covered interest arbitrage profit.

By contrast, uncovered interest arbitrage involves a borrowing in centre A for a specified period at a fixed interest rate and shipping the proceeds borrowed to centre B via the spot market. The sum is again placed on deposit for the same period as that for which the borrowing was arranged in centre A and again it is at a fixed rate. This time the investor speculates that the proceeds from lending in centre B, when shipped to centre A at the spot rate prevailing at the end of the investment period, will exceed the borrowing plus accrued interest in centre A. Note that, under uncovered interest arbitrage, the operator speculates on the future spot rate. Any profit earned is a risky profit. Under covered interest arbitrage, the operator is not speculating but making a risk-free profit based on momentary disequilibria in interest differentials and forward and spot rates.

According to the Fisher effect (see Figure 2.2), a term coined because it was observed by US economist Irving Fisher, quoted interest rates in a country reflect anticipated real returns adjusted for local inflation expectations. In a world where investors are internationally mobile, expected real rates of return should tend towards equality reflecting the fact that, in search of higher real returns, investors' arbitraging actions will force these returns towards each other. At least this should hold with respect to the free market Eurocurrency interest rates. Constraints on international capital mobility prevent this relationship from holding in domestic interest rate markets, so quoted Eurocurrency interest rates may differ for different currencies but, according to the Fisher effect, only by virtue of different inflation expectations; and these inflation differentials should underpin expected changes in the spot rates of exchange. In other words, we would expect US and UK free market interest investment to yield equal real returns. Differences in nominal returns would reflect expected inflation differentials.

We now move on to purchasing power parity. At its simplest, this theory suggests that exchange rates move to make good changes in inflation rates. Assume an example in which there are no costs of transporting goods. If the US dollar/sterling exchange rate is $1.70 and British widgets sell at £10 each, the US-produced widget should be marketed at $17 to be in line on price. If this were initially the case, and inflation in Britain and the United States amounted to 8 per cent and 4 per cent per annum, respectively, the widget prices (assuming they were to move in line with general inflation) would be £10.80 and $17.68, respectively. However, an exchange rate movement which took account of these relative inflations would ensure continuing competitiveness; such a rate would have to be $1.6370 = £1.

There are a number of reservations about purchasing power parity. First, the prices of individual goods and services rarely move exactly in line with general inflation, whether it be measured by retail prices, wholesale prices or whatever. Furthermore, the index that would be most relevant would be one based upon export prices.

The diagonal in Figure 2.2, the international Fisher effect, suggests a relationship between interest differences and expected movements of the spot exchange rate. It will be recalled that interest rate parity is based upon covered interest arbitrage. The international Fisher effect is built upon uncovered interest arbitrage. The argument is that rational investors make estimates of future spot rates of exchange. If their judgements are such as to justify excess profits from uncovered interest arbitrage, their actions in purchasing one currency and selling another will move exchange rates until such excess profits are eliminated. The effect of this speculation would be to bring interest rate differentials into line with spot exchange rates and expectations of their movement.

The test of any theory is how well it stands up in the real world. We have seen that interest rate parity is extraordinarily well supported when tested against evidence from financial markets. In the real world the Fisher effect and the international Fisher effect are found to hold in the long term, but there are substantial short-run deviations from equilibrium. Of course, if the international Fisher effect were to hold immutably, then interest rates on borrowing in different currencies would always be exactly offset by exchange rate movements. And if the Fisher effect were to hold immutably, then real interest returns (that is, quoted interest rates less expected inflation) from investment in different currencies would always be equated too.

When tested against evidence from economic statistics, purchasing power parity is found to hold up moderately well in the long term. But in the short term there are substantial deviations; so much so that using purchasing power parity as a short-term predictor of exchange rates is utterly unjustifiable. Having said this, its use as a long-run forecasting device seems better merited by the evidence. As mentioned above, purchasing power parity predicts that exchange rates change to compensate for differences in inflation between two countries. If a country's nominal exchange rate falls, and that decline is an exact compensation for inflation differentials, then its real effective exchange rate is said to remain constant. Purchasing power parity predicts that real effective exchange rates will remain constant through time.

One of the major problems with using purchasing power parity as a long-run predictive device for exchange rate forecasting is the choice of base year. Exchange rate movements may be weighted according to international trade and corrected for inflation relativities to obtain real effective exchange rates. If real effective exchange rates are indexed to 100 for the base year, it follows that for currencies where the current figure is over 100, the exchange rate is overvalued on purchasing power criteria and vice versa. But there is a problem: the answer obtained about valuation may vary according to which year is chosen as a base date.

Referring to Figure 2.3, if 1989 is used as the base year with currencies trade weighted and corrected for inflation, then by 1994, currency A appears overvalued, currency B appears correctly valued and currency C appears undervalued. But if 1992 is taken as the base year, currency A appears undervalued by 1994; at this time currency B looks overvalued and currency C looks correctly valued. So how does one get over this problem?

The answer is that one should start the analysis at a time when the exchange rate of the country being analysed is in equilibrium. And what is meant by an exchange rate being in equilibrium? One approach is to commence at a time when the exchange rate is such that the overall balance of trade plus invisibles is equal (or approximately equal) to zero. In this sense, exchange rate equilibrium may be defined as that level at which it results in the balance on trade and invisibles coming out at zero overall. However, the question of capital flows affecting exchange rate equilibrium has become so significant that a theory of fundamental equilibrium exchange rates (FEERs) has been developed. Here the notion is that the equilibrium exchange rate is that rate which is consistent with overall external balance, given underlying capital flows.

Lastly, turning to the expectations theory arm of the model outlined in Figure 2.2, the forward rate is generally (but not always) found to be an unbiased long-run predictor of the future spot rate. This means that if the forward rate is used to predict the future spot rate, the sum of gains will equal the sum of losses in the long run. But, again, there may be substantial short-term deviations.

Do these deviations show any consistency? The answer is yes. Evidence suggests that, in the short run, when a currency is substantially strengthening, the forward rate underestimates the future spot value of the strengthening currency. And, when a currency is on a significantly weakening trend, the forward rate tends to overestimate its future spot rate.

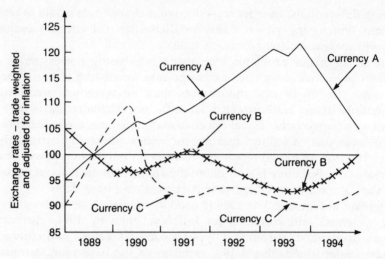

Figure 2.3 Real effective exchange rates (1989 = 100).

Practicalities

In practical treasury work, the interest rate parity side of Figure 2.2 is used in computer aids to identify whether opportunities for covered interest arbitrage exist. The international Fisher effect is resorted to in order to estimate future exchange rates implied by market interest rates in different currencies. Purchasing power parity is often used to forecast long-run foreign exchange rate movements.

In raising foreign-denominated long-term borrowings, identification of whether a currency is out of equilibrium can be a valuable exercise. All other things being equal, it is better to raise such borrowings denominated in an overvalued currency. If movements of exchange rates are towards equilibrium, there will be opportunities to repay such borrowings and make a gain in so doing.

An overview

Figure 2.2 sets out a model relating spot and forward exchange rates, interest differentials, inflation differentials and expected movements in spot. The model is most important. Indeed, in the study of foreign exchange it is perhaps the single most important set of theoretical ideas.

The model itself is an equilibrium model. In the real world markets are rarely, if ever, in equilibrium. Therefore it should not be surprising if, for lengthy periods, parts of the model do not hold in the real world. Markets move towards equilibrium and the same is true of foreign exchange markets.

But, of course, a good theory must stand up well in the real world. Evidence suggests that interest rate parity holds virtually all the time at the level of quotations to companies, but the remaining parts of the model are found to be long-run phenomena. Short-term deviations are the order of the day with the Fisher effect, purchasing power parity, the international Fisher effect and expectations theory. While this imposes threats to companies, it also creates the opportunities that were referred to in the section headed 'Practicalities'.

Appendix
A deductive proof of the four-way equivalence model

Interest rate parity

Assume that an investor has £1m to invest for a period of one year. The exchange rate quotation for the US dollar is $1.610000 spot, and $1.530949 for twelve months forward.[1] Twelve-month interest rates are $8^{15}/_{16}$ per cent for Eurodollar deposits, and $14^{9}/_{16}$ per cent for Eurosterling deposits. The investor has at least two options which avoid foreign exchange risk:

1. Invest £1m in a Eurosterling deposit at $14^{9}/_{16}$ per cent.
2. (a) Convert £1m into US dollars at $1.610000.
   (b) Invest the proceeds in a Eurodollar deposit (the point being that the deposit is a dollar deposit attracting an interest rate appropriate to dollar placements; for one year the rate is $8^{15}/_{16}$ per cent.
   (c) Sell the calculated proceeds forward one year at £1.530949.

Investing in Eurosterling, the proceeds after one year will be £1,145,625. Investing in Eurodollars the proceeds after one year may be calculated as follows:

1. The amount invested will be the spot proceeds of $1,610,000.
2. These will accumulate at $8^{15}/_{16}$ per cent to $1,753,894 after one year.
3. The sterling proceeds from selling this forward will be:

   $1,753,894 \div 1.530949 = £1,145,625$

Thus the two investment opportunities offer the same return. Were this not so, operators in the foreign exchange markets could buy in one centre, convert the money into another currency, and invest at a profit in another centre.

The actions of arbitrageurs ensure that profitable opportunities based on the above kind of operation do not last for more than very short periods. Where profitable opportunities do exist, the market would say that there are opportunities for profitable covered interest arbitrage. But exploitation of these opportunities themselves creates movements in exchange and interest rates, ensuring that the tendency in the foreign exchange market is towards equilibrium between differences in interest rates and differences between forward and spot rates.

The interest rate differential, called the *interest agio*, is calculated as:

$$\frac{i_\$ - i_£}{1 + i_£} = \frac{8^{15}\!/_{16}\% - 14^9\!/_{16}\%}{1.14^9\!/_{16}}$$

$$= -0.0491$$
$$= -4.91\%$$

Notice that calculating the interest differential precisely in this way, which is the correct method, differs from making a straight deduction:

$$i_\$ - i_£ = 8^{15}\!/_{16} - 14^9\!/_{16} = -5^5\!/_8\%$$

The annual forward premium is the *exchange agio* and is given by:

$$\frac{f_0 - s_0}{s_0} = \frac{1.530949 - 1.610000}{1.610000}$$

$$= -0.0491$$
$$= -4.91\%$$

If there are no opportunities for profitable covered interest arbitrage then the interest agio will exactly equal the exchange agio. This is the interest rate parity theorem and it is summarized in Figure 2.4. An algebraic proof of the theory is given in Figure 2.5.

Difference in interest rates		Difference between forward and spot rate
$\dfrac{i_s - i_£}{1 + i_£}$	=	$\dfrac{f_0 - s_0}{s_0}$

Figure 2.4 Interest rate parity.

A US exporter due to receive £A in one year (at time t where $t = 12$ months) might avoid foreign exchange risk in one of two ways.

Using the forward market his US dollar proceeds at time t would be \$$f_o A$. Alternatively, he could borrow £$A/(1 + i_t)$ and convert it into US dollars, giving \$$[A/(1 + i_t)]s_0$. Investing this now would yield at time t the sum of:

$$\$ \frac{A}{(1 + i_t)} s_0(1 + i_s)$$

Assuming equilibrium between money markets and foreign exchange markets, this must equal \$$f_o A$. Written mathematically:

$$\frac{A}{(1 + i_t)} s_0(1 + i_s) = f_o A$$

Dividing by A and rearranging:

$$f_0 = s_0 \frac{(1 + i_s)}{(1 + i_t)}$$

Dividing by s_0 and deducting 1:

$$\frac{f_0}{s_0} - 1 = \frac{(1 + i_s)}{(1 + i_t)} - 1$$

That is:

$$\frac{f_0 - s_0}{s_0} = \frac{(1 + i_s)}{(1 + i_t)} - 1$$

$$= \frac{(i_s - i_t)}{(1 + i_t)}$$

Figure 2.5 Interest rate parity proved.

Purchasing power parity

If a commodity sells in the US at \$300 per kilo and in the UK at £220, with the spot exchange rate at \$1.50/£, a profitable opportunity exists to buy in the USA, ship to the UK, and sell there. Arbitrageurs buying in New York and selling in London would tend to increase the US price and reduce the UK price until no profit potential existed. Within the range of costs such as shipping and insurance, the prices of an otherwise identical commodity in two centres should not differ. Thus:

£ price of commodity × \$ price of £ = \$ price of commodity

i.e.

$$\$ \text{ price of £} = \frac{\$ \text{ price of commodity}}{£ \text{ price of commodity}}$$

This kind of relationship should tend to hold for all internationally traded goods. That is

$$\text{Price of } \pounds = \frac{\$ \text{ price of an internationally traded commodity}}{\pounds \text{ price of the internationally traded commodity}}$$

Changes in the ratio of domestic prices of internationally traded goods in two centres should be reflected in changes in the price of currencies – the exchange rates.

In order to take the argument to the next stage we should, strictly speaking, limit our attention to relative prices of internationally traded goods. But we approximate. Purchasing power parity (PPP) theory uses relative general price changes as a proxy for prices of internationally traded goods. Applying it to the previous equation, we would obtain:

$$\text{Change in } \$ \text{ price of } \pounds = \frac{\text{Change in } \$ \text{ price level}}{\text{Change in } \pounds \text{ price level}}$$

Thus if inflation in the USA is 8 per cent p.a. and it is 12 per cent p.a. in the UK, then applying purchasing power parity theory we would expect the pound sterling to fall against the dollar by $(0.8 - 0.12)/1.12$, that is 3.6 per cent. Again, this calculation is precise. A quick approximation based merely on straight inflation differentials would suggest a devaluation of 4 per cent p.a. (The justification for using the precise formulation, rather than the approximate one, is considered in the algebraic formulation in Figure 2.7.)

Purchasing power parity theory, itself an approximation since it uses the general price level as a proxy for the price level for internationally traded goods, suggests that changes in the spot rate of exchange may be estimated by reference to expected inflation differentials. Figure 2.6 summarizes the purchasing power parity theorem and Figure 2.7 gives an algebraic proof.

Although simplest, then, purchasing power parity predicts that the exchange rate changes to compensate for differences in inflation between two countries. Thus, if country A has a higher inflation rate than its trading partners, the exchange rate of the former should weaken to compensate for this relativity. If country A's nominal exchange rate falls, and if that fall is an exact compensation for inflation differentials, its real effective exchange rate is said to remain constant. Purchasing power parity predicts that real effective exchange rates will remain constant through time.

The Fisher effect

According to the Fisher effect (sometimes referred to as Fisher's closed hypothesis) nominal interest rates in a country reflect anticipated real

Expected difference in inflation rates		Expected change in spot rates
$\dfrac{{}^{\bullet}p_{\$} - {}^{\bullet}p_{\pounds}}{1 + {}^{\bullet}p_{\pounds}}$	$=$	$\dfrac{{}^{\bullet}s_{t} - s_{0}}{s_{0}}$

Figure 2.6 Purchasing power parity.

Given that relative price levels underpin the spot rate of exchange at any date, the values of the spot rate now and the expected spot rate at time t are given respectively by:

$$s_0 = \frac{p_{\$}}{p_{\pounds}} \quad \text{and} \quad {}^{\bullet}s_t = \frac{p_{\$}(1 + {}^{\bullet}p_{\$})}{p_{\pounds}(1 + {}^{\bullet}p_{\pounds})}$$

Subtracting these two equations:

$$ {}^{\bullet}s_t - s_0 = \frac{p_{\$}}{p_{\pounds}} \left[\frac{(1 + {}^{\bullet}p_{\$})}{(1 + {}^{\bullet}p_{\pounds})} - 1 \right]$$

Dividing by s_0 (which is the equivalent of multiplying by $p_{\pounds}/p_{\$}$)

$$\frac{{}^{\bullet}s_t - s_0}{s_0} = \frac{{}^{\bullet}p_{\$} - {}^{\bullet}p_{\pounds}}{1 + {}^{\bullet}p_{\pounds}}$$

Figure 2.7 Purchasing power parity proved.

returns adjusted for local inflation expectations. In a world where investors are internationally mobile, expected real rates of return should tend towards equality, reflecting the fact that in search of higher real returns, investors' arbitraging actions will force these returns towards each other. At least, this should hold with respect to the free market Eurocurrency interest rates. Constraints on international capital mobility create imperfections which, among other things, prevent this relationship from holding in domestic interest rate markets. So nominal Eurocurrency interest rates may differ for different currencies but, according to the Fisher effect, only by virtue of different inflation expectations. And, these inflation differentials should underpin expected changes in the spot rates of exchange. In other words, we would expect US and UK free market interest investment to yield equal real returns. Differences in nominal returns would reflect expected inflation differentials. This would give us the Fisher effect theorem summarized in Figure 2.8 and proved using elementary mathematics in Figure 2.9.

Difference in interest rates		Expected difference in inflation rates
$\dfrac{i_s - i_{\mathfrak{L}}}{1 + i_f}$	=	$\dfrac{{}^{\bullet}p_s - {}^{\bullet}p_{\mathfrak{L}}}{1 + {}^{\bullet}p_{\mathfrak{L}}}$

Figure 2.8 The Fisher effect.

Local interest rates will equal the international real return (r) adjusted for expected local inflation. Thus:

$$1 + i_s = (1 + r)(1 + {}^{\bullet}p_s) \quad and \quad 1 + i_{\mathfrak{L}} = (1 + r)(1 + {}^{\bullet}p_{\mathfrak{L}})$$

Subtracting these two equations:

$$i_s - i_{\mathfrak{L}} = (1 + r)({}^{\bullet}p_s - {}^{\bullet}p_{\mathfrak{L}})$$

Dividing by $(1 + r)$:

$$\frac{i_s - i_{\mathfrak{L}}}{1 + r} = {}^{\bullet}p_s - {}^{\bullet}p_{\mathfrak{L}}$$

Dividing by $(1 + {}^{\bullet}p_{\mathfrak{L}})$:

$$\frac{i_s - i_{\mathfrak{L}}}{1 + i_{\mathfrak{L}}} = \frac{{}^{\bullet}p_s - {}^{\bullet}p_{\mathfrak{L}}}{1 + {}^{\bullet}p_{\mathfrak{L}}}$$

Figure 2.9 The Fisher effect proved.

Expectations theory

We have already demonstrated the following equivalues:

Differences between forward and spot rates	= Differences in interest rates
Differences in interest rates	= Differences in expected inflation rates
Differences in expected inflation rates	= Expected change in spot rate

By logic it follows that the difference between the forward and spot rates equals the expected change in the spot rate. This is the expectations theory of exchange rates.

Expectations Theory	
Difference between forward and spot rates	Expected change in spot rate
$\dfrac{f_0 - s_0}{s_0}$	$\dfrac{{}^{\bullet}s_t - s_0}{s_0}$

with $=$ centered between the two fractions.

Figure 2.10 Expectations theory.

If users of the foreign exchange market were not interested in risk, then the forward rate of exchange would depend solely on what people expected the future spot rate to be. A twelve-month forward rate of $1.530949 to the pound would exist only because traders expected the spot rate in twelve months to be $1.530949 to the pound. If they anticipated that it would be higher than this, nobody would sell sterling at the forward rate. By the same token, if they expected it to be lower, nobody would buy at the forward rate.

If traders do care about risk, the forward rate might be higher or lower than the expected spot rate. Suppose that a US exporter is certain to receive £1m in six months' time, he might wait until six months have elapsed then convert to dollars or he might sell the pound forward. The first action involves exchange risk; the latter does not. To avoid foreign exchange risk, the trader may be willing to pay something slightly different from the expected spot price.

On the other side of the equation, there may be traders who wish to buy sterling six months away. To avoid the risk associated with movements in foreign exchange rates, they may be prepared to pay a forward price a little higher than the expected spot price.

Some traders find it safer to sell sterling forward; some traders find it safer to buy sterling forward. If the former group predominates, the forward price of sterling is likely to be less than the expected spot price. If the latter group predominates, the forward price is likely to be greater than the expected spot price. The actions of the predominant group are likely to adjust rates until they arrive at the hypothesized position in Figure 2.10.

The international Fisher effect

The hypothesis that differences in interest rate should underpin the expected movement in the spot rate of exchange is termed the international Fisher effect; it is sometimes also called Fisher's open hypothesis. Again, it follows by logic from the equivalences already proved and it is shown as the diagonal in Figure 2.2.

Four-way equivalence in the foreign exchange market

We can now combine the separate relationships we have been discussing to show the four-way equivalence in the foreign exchange market. This relationship is summarized in Figure 2.2.

Note

1. The foreign exchange market quotes the US dollar sterling to four decimal places. In this appendix the quotation is to six places to explain more clearly the principles involved.

3

How are foreign exchange rates quoted?

The foreign exchange market is the framework of individuals, firms, banks and brokers who buy and sell foreign currencies. The foreign exchange market for any one currency, for example the French franc, consists of all the locations such as Paris, London, New York, Zurich, Frankfurt and so on, in which the French franc is bought and sold for other currencies. Foreign exchange markets tend to be located in national financial centres near the local financial markets. The most important foreign exchange markets are found in London, New York, Tokyo, Frankfurt, Amsterdam, Paris, Zurich, Toronto, Brussels, Milan, Singapore and Hong Kong.

There are four main types of transaction undertaken in these foreign exchange markets: spot transactions, forward deals, futures transactions and currency options.

In the spot market, currencies are bought and sold for immediate delivery. In practice, this means that settlement is made two working days after the spot date. The intervention of these two days allows for necessary paperwork to be completed. In the forward market, currencies are bought and sold at prices agreed now but for future delivery at an agreed date. Not only is delivery made in the future, but payment is also made at the future date.

The players

The main participants in the market are companies and individuals, commercial banks, central banks and brokers. Companies and individuals need foreign currency for business or travel reasons. Commercial banks are the source from which companies and individuals obtain their foreign currency. Through their extensive network of dealing rooms, their arbitrage operations (buying in one centre and selling in another), banks ensure that quotations in different centres tend towards the same price.

There are also foreign exchange brokers who bring buyers, sellers and banks together and receive commissions on deals arranged. The other main player operating in the market is the central bank, the main part of whose foreign exchange activities involves the buying and selling of the home currency or foreign currencies with a view to ensuring that the exchange rate moves in line with established targets set for it by the government.

Not only are there numerous foreign exchange market centres around the world, but dealers in different locations can communicate with one another via the telephone, telex and computers. The overlapping of time zones means that, apart from weekends, there is always one centre that is open.

Methods of quotation

A foreign exchange rate is the price of one currency in terms of another. Foreign exchange dealers quote two prices, one for selling, one for buying. The first area of mystique in foreign exchange quotations arises from the fact that there are two ways of quoting rates: the direct quote and the indirect quote. The former gives the quotation in terms of the number of units of home currency necessary to buy one unit of foreign currency. The latter gives the quotation in terms of the number of units of foreign currency bought with one unit of home currency.

Continental European dealers normally quote via the direct method. In London dealers use the indirect method. In the USA, both quotation methods are used. When a bank is dealing with a customer within the USA a direct quotation is given, but when dealing with other banks in Europe (except the UK), the indirect quotation is used.

Foreign exchange dealers quote two prices: the rate at which they are prepared to sell a currency and that at which they are prepared to buy. The difference between the bid rate and the offer is the dealer's spread which is one of the potential sources of profit for dealers. Whether using the direct quotation method or the indirect quote, the smaller rate is always termed the bid rate and the higher is called the offer, or ask, rate.

If we assume that the middle quote (that is, halfway between the sell and buy price) for Deutsche Marks to the US dollar is DM1.3753 = $1, then the New York internal quote for this rate would be $0.7271 and the Frankfurt quote would be DM1.3753. Where both centres use the same method of quotation (that is, they both use the direct quote or they both use the indirect method) and when they are both in effect quoting the same price (in other words there are no arbitrage opportunities) the quote in one centre is the reciprocal of the other. Thus the two quotes multiplied together will equal 1.0. To the extent that this condition fails to hold, possibilities for profitable arbitrage (selling in one centre and buying in the other) exist. Of course, operators need to look at the buy rate in one centre and the sell rate in the other in terms of assessing arbitrage opportunities. In carrying out a profitable arbitrage, dealers force the prices in various centres towards equality.

If, in terms of the middle quote, the sterling/US dollar rate is $1.6015 equals £1, then the New York quote (using the local direct method) will be $1.6015 and the London quote (using the indirect method) will also be $1.6015. Where one centre uses the direct quotation method and the other uses the indirect method, the two quotations will, assuming no profitable arbitrage opportunities exist, be exactly the same.

The size of the bid/offer spread varies according to the depth of the market and its stability at any particular time. Depth of a market refers to the volume of transactions in a particular currency. Deep markets have many deals; shallow markets have few. High percentage spreads are associated with high uncertainty (perhaps due to impending devaluation) and low volumes of transactions in a currency. Lower spreads are associated with stable, high-volume markets. Deep markets usually have narrower spreads than shallow ones.

If US dollars are quoted in terms of sterling as $1.6050 to $1.6060, it means that the dealer is prepared to sell dollars at $1.6050 to the pound, or buy dollars at $1.6060. Conversely, the dealer is prepared to buy pounds at the rate of $1.6050 or sell pounds at $1.6060. In the above example, the spread is equal to $0.0010, or 10 points. A point (or pip, as it is widely referred to) is a unit of a decimal, usually the fourth place to the right of the decimal point.

Next, it is necessary to consider the meaning of cross rates. A cross rate may be defined as an exchange rate which is calculated from two (or more) other rates. Thus the rate for the Deutsche Mark to the Swedish krona will be derived as the cross rate from the US dollar to the Deutsche Mark and the US dollar to the krona.

The practice in world foreign exchange markets is that currencies are quoted against the US dollar. If one bank asks another for its Deutsche Mark rate, that rate will be quoted against the US dollar unless otherwise specified. Most dealings are done against the US dollar, hence it follows that the market rate for a currency at any moment is most accurately reflected in its exchange rate against the US dollar. A bank that was asked to quote sterling against the Swiss franc would normally do so by calculating this rate from the £/US$ rate and the US$/SFr rate. It would therefore be using cross rates to arrive at its quotation.

Let us suppose that we require a quote for Swiss francs against the Deutsche Mark. The quotation which we would receive would be derived through the quote of both currencies against the US dollar.

If these rates against the dollar were US$1 = SFr1.1326/1.1336 and US$1 = DM1.3750/1.3755, it would be possible to derive the cross rate for the Swiss franc against the Deutsche Mark. Our goal is to derive the selling and buying rates for Swiss francs in terms of Deutsche Marks. If we are selling Swiss francs we will be buying Deutsche Marks. So we begin with the rate for selling Swiss francs and buying dollars; we then move to selling dollars and buying Deutsche Marks. The amalgamation of these two rates gives us the rate for selling Swiss francs and buying Deutsche Marks. The rate for selling Swiss francs to the dealer and buying dollars is SFr1.1336; the rate for selling dollars and buying Deutsche Marks is DM1.3750. So selling SFr1 gives $0.8822. Selling $0.8822 gives DM1.2130. Thus the rate for selling Swiss francs and buying Deutsche Marks is SFr1 = DM1.2130, or DM1 = SFr0.8244.

Similarly, in our example, if we are buying Swiss francs we will be selling Deutsche Marks. This time we begin with the rate for buying Swiss francs from the dealer and selling dollars to him, and then we move to buying dollars and selling Deutsche Marks. Amalgamating these two rates gives us the rate for buying Swiss francs and selling Deutsche Marks. The rate for buying Swiss francs and selling dollars is SFr1.1326; the rate for buying dollars and selling Deutsche Marks is DM1.3755. Selling DM1 gives $0.7270. Selling $0.7270 gives SFr0.8234. Thus the rate for buying Swiss francs and selling Deutsche Marks is DM1 = SFr0.8234, or SFr1 = DM1.2145. Thus the cross rate quotation using direct Zurich figures would be SFr0.8234/0.8244 = DM1, and the direct Frankfurt quote would be DM1.2130/1.2145.

Forward contracts and quotations

It is necessary to consider next how forward rates are quoted by foreign exchange dealers. A forward foreign exchange contract is an agreement between two parties to exchange one currency for another at some future date. The rate at which the exchange is to be made, the delivery date and the amounts involved are fixed at the time of the agreement.

One of the major problems that newcomers to foreign exchange markets have is understanding how the forward premium and discount works and how foreign exchange dealers quote for forward delivery. Assume that a quoted currency is more expensive in the future than it is now in terms of the base currency. The quoted currency is then said to stand at a premium in the forward market relative to the base currency. Conversely, the base currency is said to stand at a discount relative to the quoted currency.

Consider an example in which the US dollar is the base currency and the Deutsche Mark is the quoted currency. Assume that the spot rate is US$1 = DM1.3753. The rate quoted by a bank today for delivery in three months' time (today's three-month forward rate) is US$1 = DM1.3748. In this example, the dollar buys fewer Deutsche Marks in three months' time than it does today. So the Deutsche Mark is more expensive in the forward market. Thus the dollar stands at a discount relative to the Deutsche Mark; conversely, the Deutsche Mark stands at a premium relative to the dollar. The size of the dollar discount or Deutsche Mark premium is the difference between 1.3753 and 1.3748, that is, 0.05 pfennigs. The convention in the foreign exchange market is frequently to quote in terms of points, or hundredths of a unit. Hence 0.05 pfennigs is frequently quoted as 5 points.

In order to arrive at the forward prices, the Deutsche Mark premium or dollar discount must be subtracted from the spot rate. Were there a Deutsche Mark discount or dollar premium, this would be added to the spot rate. But care has to be taken: in our example we used a New York indirect quote. Had we used a New York direct quote, the reverse would apply: in other words, the Deutsche Mark premium or dollar discount would have to be added to the spot quotation. An easier way to deal with this little problem is always to remember (and this has never, in practice, been found to be otherwise) that the bid/offer spread on the forward quote is always wider than the spread on the spot figure. If this is remembered it is an easy process to compare the two spreads and, if the forward spread is narrower than the spot spread, the sums have been done incorrectly and recomputation is necessary.

Just as in the spot market, dealers quote selling and buying rates in the forward market, too. As in the spot market the convention, whether using direct or indirect quotation methods, is that the smaller rate is quoted first. In the above example the spot rate for Deutsche Mark to US dollar might be quoted as DM1.3748/1.3758 and the three-month Deutsche Mark premium (or dollar discount) might be 6/3. Thus, if the foreign exchange dealer is buying dollars forward, there will be a Deutsche Mark premium of 6 points, or 0.06 pfennigs. But if he is buying the Deutsche Mark, the premium will only be 3 points or 0.03 pfennigs. Using the convention that the forward spread is wider than the spot spread, the full three-month forward quotation comes out at DM1.7069/1.7082.

	Bid rate	Offer rate	Spread in points
Spot quotation	1.3748	1.3758	10
Forward spread	6	3	3
Subtract to make forward spread 13 points	1.3742	1.3755	13

Sometimes forward quotes are given as −10/+10 or 10P10. In this situation the forward market is said to be 'round par'. Thus, to get the forward rate, 10 points have to be added to either the bid or offer and 10 points have to be subtracted so that the forward spread widens on the spot spread. For example, take the quotations of:

1.3748/1.3758 − 10/ + 10

The forward rate could be construed as 1.3738/1.3768, i.e. it may be quoted in full rather than as points distance from spot. This is called the outright forward price. It would be computed as:

	Bid rate	Offer rate	Spread in points
Spot quotation	1.3748	1.3758	10
Forward spread	(10)	10	20
	1.3738	1.3768	30

Sometimes this kind of situation is quoted in terms of the spread from the spot rate as 10 pfennigs discount, 10 pfennigs premium.

It is important to bear in mind that the currency quoted at a discount in the forward market relative to another currency will have higher Eurocurrency interest rates than the currency which is at the premium. The rationale for this was discussed in the previous chapter.

As an adjunct to the above methods of quoting forward foreign exchange rates, we sometimes see the percentage per annum cost of forward cover. What does this mean and how is it calculated? The annualized forward premium may be expressed as a percentage by reference to the formula:

$$\frac{\text{Forward rate} - \text{Spot rate}}{\text{Spot rate}} \times \frac{12}{n} \times 100$$

where n is the number of months in the forward contract. It should be noted that small differences in the annual percentage cost of forward cover arise when using the direct quotation method as opposed to using the indirect quote. Slightly different results also arise from using the buying rate as opposed to the selling rate or the middle price. The problem of differing costs of forward cover for buying and selling is easily resolved. While different figures are achieved using mathematics, the relevant figure for a company executive using the forward market is the percentage cost of doing the transaction that he or she wishes to undertake.

Let us look at an example. Suppose again that we have a spot rate

of US$1 = DM1.3748/1.3758 and that the three-month forward quote
is 6/3. The forward rate came out (see above) as DM1.3742/1.3755. If
we were a buyer of Deutsche Marks forward, the forward premium
would be obtained by comparing the rates for buying Deutsche Marks
(that is DM1.3748 spot and DM1.3742 three months forward). The
annualized forward premium for buying Deutsche Marks would therefore
amount to:

$$\frac{1.3742 - 1.3748}{1.3748} \times \frac{12}{3} \times 100 = -0.17\% \text{ p.a.}$$

The Deutsche Mark is said to be at an annualized premium of 0.17 per
cent in the three-month forward market based on rates for buying
marks.

An overview

Foreign exchange markets comprise the framework of individuals, firms,
banks and brokers who buy and sell foreign currencies. Market participants
include companies, individuals, commercial banks, central banks and
brokers. Between 90 and 95 per cent of all foreign exchange transactions
involve banks on both sides of the deal. Trade accounts for only 1 or 2
per cent of all transactions nowadays.

Time zones around the world overlap, hence the foreign exchange
markets are in effect open all the time in one centre or another, except at
weekends. The sinews of this chapter concern the ways in which the
financial community quotes foreign exchange rates. An investment of time
here will be amply repaid as progress is made through the field of
international money.

4

What makes exchange rates move?

Explanations of economic phenomena often conflict. Hypotheses are advanced and tested. For a while it looks as if one particular series of explanatory variables is accounting for changes in the dependent variable – then the relationship breaks down. We should not be too surprised at the infuriatingly unpredictable way in which the economic world seems to work.

International money is no exception. The key questions to which we seek a solution are what makes foreign exchange rates move and can these movements be predicted? We are looking for a regression equation in which the future spot rate is the dependent variable and there may be one or more independent variables whose coefficients can be estimated with, it might be hoped, acceptably high levels of significance and reliability.

Unfortunately the models that have been developed do not necessarily hold for anything but quite short periods. We simply do not have the kind of model which can be relied upon with high degrees of certainty in terms of predicting movements in spot exchange rates. So what are the competing hypotheses, and can we do anything about predicting movements in foreign exchange rates?

In Chapter 2, purchasing power parity was briefly covered. This is one model developed to explain and predict exchange rate movements. However, it is shown empirically to work over long periods rather than over the short term. The fact that short-term deviations from purchasing power parity abound has stimulated the search for a better model: one of these is the balance of payments approach.

The balance of payments approach

In its original form, the balance of payments explanation tended to ignore capital flows. The current account theory can best be explained by approaching it under the two distinct systems of exchange rate regime: fixed and floating.

30

Assume a fixed exchange rate system first. Economic models suggest that the current account gets worse as national income rises. The tendency is for the domestic currency to weaken to pay for the increased imports. The fixed exchange rate system requires that, should this pressure move beyond certain narrow exchange rate limits, this should be countered by support from the domestic government. This might take the form of selling reserves of foreign currency in the foreign exchange markets. Usually this would be accompanied by domestic severity to dampen home demand, possibly witnessed through a lower relative money supply growth with consequent lower relative inflation leading to an improvement in exports and a lowering of imports. According to this formula the current account deficit is automatically corrected.

The same applies to a surplus. Here, rather than selling foreign exchange reserves, the foreign currency is bought. To pay for this, borrowings are increased – probably by the issue of treasury bills. Being a reserve asset this results in an increase in money supply which in turn leads, all other things being equal, to higher inflation. Remember we are looking at a fixed parity regime. This means that exports become less competitive hence the surplus reduces: again, an automatic corrective mechanism.

On paper, then, the fixed exchange rate system should have avoided permanent disequilibria: there are automatically correcting means of achieving current account stability at work. In the real world, though, things did not turn out this way, as anyone who has examined the evidence of Britain in the 1950s and 1960s knows. And the test of a theory is how well it works in reality.

We now turn to the current account theory of exchange rates under a floating currency regime. Again, in terms of illustrating the mechanism, let us begin from an increase in national income and a worsening of the current account balance. We will again leave the capital account out of the equation for now. Paying for the increased imports results in demand for foreign currency at the expense of the home currency. Buying foreign exchange for domestic currency weakens the local currency which then makes exports more competitive and consequently improves the current account. By a reverse argument, current account surpluses recede as the exchange rate strengthens, again bringing about an automatic correction.

Our models, so far, have been simplistic to the extent that the capital account and the interest rate have been left out of the equation. Extending the argument to make good this omission, a slightly different model is obtained. The overall balance of payments is the current account plus the capital account. Again, we use a simple example to illustrate the workings of the model. Let us begin by assuming an increase in national income with an accompanying deterioration in the current account balance. If overall balance of payments equilibrium is to be maintained at zero as national income increases, the domestic real rate of interest must also rise – this improves capital flows to compensate for the initial deterioration in the current account. This increase in the interest rate dampens domestic demand which, in its turn, has the effect of reducing imports and consequently improves the current account.

The mechanism of this version of the balance-of-payments model involves the interest rate increase as a means of avoiding a weakening in the domestic currency. This is in line with conventional wisdom – but does not accord with the monetary approach.

The monetary approach

In the world of classical economics, trade deficits were associated directly with money supply changes. In its more modern form, the monetary approach predicts that an excess supply of money domestically will be reflected in an outflow across the foreign exchanges.

Let us start from our example of a growth in national income. Under the monetary approach, this is associated with a growing demand for money with which to carry out the increased size and volume of transactions. The resultant demand for money can be met in one of two ways: through domestic credit expansion or through a balance of payments surplus. Fast real growth causes a growth in transactions demand for money. The economy induces an inflow of money via the balance of payments to the extent that this money is not created by the central bank. This theory explains why fast-growing economies like West Germany and Japan have demonstrated almost perpetual balance of payments current account surpluses. Remember, the Keynesian model predicts that an increase in national income will be associated with a weakening current account balance. As the reader is probably well aware, we often find conflicting economic explanations of real world phenomena; this generally means that we are not completely sure of cause and effect.

Assuming that two countries have equal real growth but that one increases its money supply more than the other, logical reasoning would suggest that relative interest rates and expected relative inflations would alter. The economy with the high relative money supply growth should have a weakening exchange rate. According to the monetary approach, high interest rates and weakening currencies both flow from high relative money supply growth.

So far we have looked at some economic explanations of exchange rate movements. In reality there are many more which are beyond the scope of this introductory text. Empirical tests indicate that we would not be well advised to risk large amounts of money on short-term forecasts based solely on econometric models. Over the near term, chartist models seem to perform better in the world of foreign exchange markets. There seem to be plenty of forecasters of exchange rates who rely on chart methods. So how do charts work in terms of forecasting prices?

Chartism

Applied to share price movements, commodity price movements and currencies, this technique involves the study of past price movements to seek out potential future trends. Implicit in this possibility is the assumption that past price patterns provide a guide to future movements.

For readers unfamiliar with what chartism (sometimes called technical analysis) does, this section gives a very brief description. Chartists aim to predict share price movements by assuming that past price patterns will be repeated. There is no true theoretical justification for this. Chartists do not attempt to predict every price change. They are more interested in trends and trend reversals (when the price of a share or commodity has been rising for several months but suddenly starts to fall). Features of chartism that are considered important for predicting trend reversals include:

1. The observance of resistance levels.
2. Head and shoulders patterns.
3. Double bottom or double top patterns.

But there is a great deal more, too; all that can be done here is to give a flavour. The main features referred to can best be illustrated by examples.

Referring to Figure 4.1, the dotted line represents the lower resistance level on a rising trend. It will be noted that many of the troughs lie on this line, but only at the end is it breached. The chartist would tend to view this breach as an indication that the trend had been reversed.

In Figure 4.2 the basic trend has been flat with oscillations within a channel. There are upper and lower resistance levels which bound this channel and, according to chartists, the breach of either of these will indicate a new trend. This sort of pattern arises from market indecision, as does the triangular pattern in Figure 4.3. In this exhibit the breach of the resistance lines is said to indicate a change of trend.

Let us now look at a resistance level signalled by a double top. Suppose that the price of a share has been rising steadily for some time. Recently

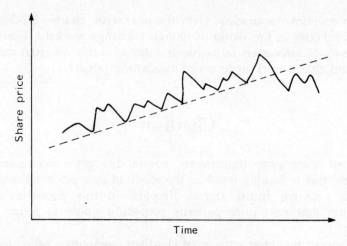

Figure 4.1 Breach of a rising bend.

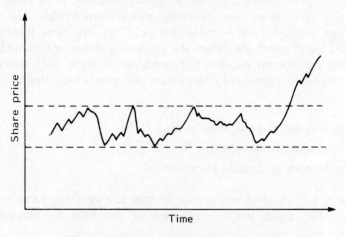

Figure 4.2 Movement out of a channel.

the price has fallen as some investors have sold in order to realize profits. It then rose again to its maximum level for a second time before starting to fall again. This is known as a double top and, based on experience, the chartist would predict that the trend has reversed. A typical double top might appear as shown in Figure 4.4. Double bottoms are interpreted in a similar – but reverse – way.

Another indication of a trend reversal is the head and shoulders formation of the type shown in Figure 4.5. In this kind of situation the chart might be interpreted as follows. The price has been rising for some

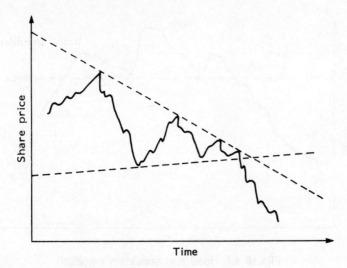

Figure 4.3 Breach of triangular pattern.

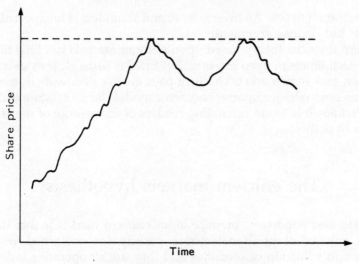

Figure 4.4 Double top formation.

time. At the peak of the left shoulder, profit-taking has caused the price to drop. The price has then risen steeply again to the head before more profit-taking causes the price to drop to around the same level as before – the neck. Although the price rises again, the gains are not as great as at the head. The level of the right shoulder together with the dips down to the neck suggests to the chartist that the upward trend previously observed is over and that a fall is imminent. The breach of the neckline

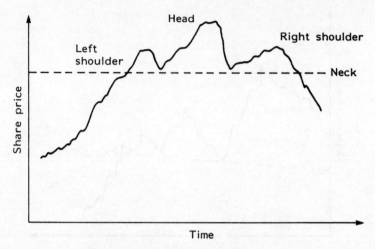

Figure 4.5 Head and shoulders formation.

is the indication to sell. An inverse head and shoulders is interpreted using a similar but reverse argument.

Modern financial theory based upon efficient markets has little time for chartist techniques in deep markets. But there is some clear evidence that in foreign exchange markets chartism pays greater dividends in the short term than does reliance upon econometric models for forecasting exchange rates. Perhaps it is worth reminding readers of the essence of the efficient markets hypothesis.

The efficient markets hypothesis

An initial, and important, premise of an efficient market is that there is a large number of profit-maximizing participants concerned with the analysis and valuation of securities and they are all operating independently of one another. A second assumption is that new information regarding securities comes to the market in a random fashion. The third assumption of an efficient market is especially crucial: investors adjust security prices rapidly to reflect the effect of new information. While the price adjustments made are not always perfect, they are unbiased. In other words, sometimes there is an over-adjustment, sometimes there is an under-adjustment; it is unknown which it will be. Adjustment of security prices takes place rapidly because the market is dominated by profit maximizing investors. The combined effects of new information coming to market participants in a random, independent fashion plus the presence of numerous investors who adjust stock prices rapidly to reflect this new information means, according to efficient market theorists, that price changes are likely to be independent and random. According to chartism, of course, price changes are not independent – they are to some extent a function of past price movements. It is evident why efficient market proponents utterly reject the claims of chartists.

In our brief overview of efficient markets it should be mentioned that, because security prices adjust to all new information and supposedly reflect all public information at any point in time, the security prices that prevail in the market should be an unbiased reflection of all currently available information.

Based on this brief description, an efficient market is evidently one in which security prices adjust rapidly to the infusion of new information, and current stock prices fully reflect all available information, including the risk involved. It follows that the expected returns implicit in a security's price reflect merely the anticipated risk involved. The expected return on a security is consistent with risk – nothing more. Our excursion into the essence of efficient markets theory cannot be complete without reference to the three gradations of efficient market: the weak form, the semi-strong and the strong form.

The weak form of efficient market hypothesis assumes that current stock prices fully reflect all stock market information including the sequence of prices in the past, price changes and any volume information. Because current prices already reflect all past price changes and any other stock market information, this implies that there should be no relationship between past price changes and future price changes. That is, price changes are independent of any trading rule – like chartism – that depends upon past price changes. In other words, past market data cannot be of any use in predicting future prices.

The semi-strong form of efficient market asserts that security prices adjust rapidly to the release of all new public information. In short, stock prices fully reflect all publicly available data. Obviously the semi-strong hypothesis encompasses the weak form hypothesis because all public information includes all market information such as past stock prices, trends and so on plus all non-market information such as earnings, stock splits, economic news, political news and so forth. A direct implication of this hypothesis is that investors acting on important new information after it is public cannot derive above-average profits from the transaction because the security price already reflects the effects of this new information. It is the security analyst's job to ensure that the implications of information for share prices are taken into account. To the extent that they are not, a buy or sell recommendation is issued to dealers and institutions which will result in price movements such that the market quote does take on board the public information.

The strong form efficient market hypothesis contends that stock prices fully reflect all information – whether public or otherwise. Hence, it implies that no group of investors has a monopolistic access to information relevant to the formation of security prices. Therefore, no group of investors should be able consistently to derive above-average profits. The strong form hypothesis encompasses both the weak and semi-strong forms. Further, the strong form hypothesis requires not only efficient markets, where prices adjust rapidly to the release of new public information, but also it requires perfect markets in which all information is available to everyone at the same time. This form of the efficient market hypothesis contends that because all information is immediately available to everyone and is rapidly discounted by everyone, no group has monopolistic access to important new information and, therefore, no individual trader can consistently derive anything more than the average profits for all traders.

For first line stocks quoted on the International Stock Exchange in London, the market exhibits efficiency in the semi-strong sense. But our concern here is with foreign exchange markets. It will be recalled that at the beginning of the discussion of the efficient market hypothesis the basic premise of an efficient market was that there should be a large number of profit-maximizing participants. So there are in the foreign exchange markets. But there are also very large non-profit-maximizers; indeed, the largest players are not profit-maximizers. The largest players are the central banks whose intervention is designed not to make profits but to ease currency price movements. Through intervention, they aim to achieve a multiplicity of political objectives. The question is whether this intervention stops currency markets from exhibiting market efficiency. This is entirely an empirical question. To summarize the evidence, it is conflicting. The markets in some currencies exhibit efficiency some of the time, but not all of the time. Probably this is because central banks intervene some of the time only. One opinion is that governments' direct intervention in foreign exchange markets and via the levels of interest rates is so great that currency markets cannot, from a deductive standpoint, be expected to exhibit all of the characteristics of market efficiency with anything like consistency. The corollary of which is that chartism may well pay off in the foreign exchange markets some of the time.

An overview

Students of international money have long asked whether there is any single model which can be relied upon for the purpose of predicting movements in exchange rates. Such students are seeking a deductive model which when tested in the real world stands up to statistical rigour. Unfortunately the models that have been developed do not seem to hold in anything like a reliable and consistent way, so we do not have the sort of model which can be relied upon with high degrees of certainty in terms of predicting movements in exchange rates. What we do have is a series of competing hypotheses. This chapter has presented the sinews of the competing hypotheses and summarized some of the evidence about their reliability.

5

What is foreign exchange risk?

Foreign exchange risk management begins by identifying what items and amounts a firm has exposed to risk associated with changes in exchange rates. An asset, liability, profit or expected future cash flow stream (whether certain or not) is said to be exposed to exchange risk when a currency movement would change, for better or worse, its parent or home currency value. The term exposure used in the context of foreign exchange means that a firm has assets, liabilities, profits or expected future cash flow streams such that the home currency value of assets, liabilities, profits or the present value in home currency terms of expected future cash flows changes as exchange rates change. Risk arises because currency movements may alter home currency values.

In this sense, assets, liabilities and expected future cash flow streams denominated in foreign currencies are clearly exposed to foreign exchange risk. But some expected future cash flows denominated in home currency terms may also be exposed. For example, a UK company selling in its home market may be competing with firms based in Germany. In such circumstances changes in the Deutsche Mark/sterling exchange rate will almost certainly affect the present value of the UK company's expected cash flows by strengthening or weakening its competitive position against its German rivals.

Foreign exchange exposure is usually categorized according to whether it falls into one or more of the following categories.

1. Transaction exposure.
2. Translation exposure.
3. Economic exposure.

Transaction exposure arises because a payable or receivable is denominated in a foreign currency. Translation exposure arises on the consolidation of foreign currency denominated assets and liabilities in the process of preparing consolidated accounts. This concept is essentially concerned, then, with what might be called accounting exposure. Economic exposure arises because the present value of a stream of expected future operating cash flows denominated in the home currency or in a foreign currency may vary due to changed exchange rates. Transaction and economic exposure are both cash flow exposures. Transaction exposure is a comparatively straightforward concept but translation and economic exposure are more complex. Each of the three categories of exposure is now examined and defined in more detail.

Transaction exposure

Transaction exposure arises because the cost or proceeds (in home currency) of settlement of a future payment or receipt denominated in a currency other than the home currency may vary due to changes in exchange rates. Clearly, transaction exposure is a cash flow exposure. It may be associated with trading flows (such as foreign currency denominated trade debtors and trade creditors), dividend flows or capital flows (such as foreign currency denominated dividends or loan repayments).

Translation exposure

Consolidation of financial statements which involve foreign currency denominated assets and liabilities automatically gives rise to translation exposure, sometimes termed accounting exposure. Consolidation of foreign subsidiaries' accounts into group financial statements denominated in home currency requires the application of a rate or rates of exchange to foreign subsidiaries' accounts, in order that they may be translated into the parent currency. Both balance sheets and income statements must be consolidated, and they both give rise to translation exposure. Translating foreign currency profit and loss accounts at either the average exchange rate during the accounting year or at the exchange rate at the end of the accounting year (both methods are currently permissible British accounting procedures) will mean that expected consolidated profit will vary as the average or the expected closing rate changes. So the whole amount of profit earned in foreign currency is exposed to translation risk in the sense that the home currency consolidated profit may vary as exchange rates vary.

Balance sheet exposure is somewhat more complex. Some items in a foreign subsidiary's balance sheet may be translated at their historical exchange rates (the rate prevailing at the date of acquisition or any subsequent revaluation). Thus their home currency translated value cannot alter as exchange rates alter; such assets and liabilities are not exposed in the accounting sense. Other items may be translated at the closing exchange rate – the rate prevailing at the balance sheet date at the end of the accounting period. While the value of such items is fixed in the foreign subsidiary's currency, the amount translated into the parent currency will alter as the exchange rate alters. Hence all foreign currency items which are consolidated at current rates are exposed in the accounting sense.

Accounting exposure, therefore, reflects the possibility that foreign currency denominated items which are consolidated into group published financial statements at current or average rates will show a translation loss or gain as a result. This kind of exposure does not give an indication of the true effects of currency fluctuations on a company's foreign operations.

Economic exposure, to be discussed later, is a far better measure of true value exposure. Translation exposure, as will become clear later, is really a function of the system of accounting for foreign assets and liabilities on consolidation which a group of companies uses. Clearly, it has little to do with true value in an economic sense.

There are four basic translation methods. These are the current/non-current method (sometimes called the traditional or working capital method), the all current (or closing rate) method, the monetary/non-monetary method, and the temporal method. These differing means of translation are considered in detail below. It is worth mentioning that the all current method is now the most frequently used in Britain, the USA and many other countries.

The current/non-current method
This approach uses the traditional accounting distinction between current and long-term items and translates the former at the closing rate and the latter at the historical rate. Accounting exposure for a foreign subsidiary at a particular point in time is given by the net figure of assets less liabilities that are exposed to potential change should exchange rates alter. Evidently, according to the current/non-current method, the sum exposed is net current assets.

One of the implications of this method of translation is that inventory is exposed to foreign exchange risk but long-term debt is not. The logic of such an assumption is by no means apparent. Indeed, it should be clear that long-term debt is very much exposed to exchange risk. In home currency terms, the cash amount of a foreign-currency denominated loan (whether a payable or receivable loan) will change as exchange rates change. This lack of logic underpins the move away from the current/non-current method which has been witnessed over recent years.

The all current (closing rate) method
This method merely translates all foreign currency denominated items at the closing rate of exchange. Accounting exposure is given simply by net assets or shareholders' funds (sometimes called equity). This method has become increasingly popular over time and is now the major worldwide method of translating foreign subsidiaries' balance sheets.

The monetary/non-monetary method
Monetary items are assets, liabilities or capital, the amounts of which are fixed by contract in terms of the number of currency units regardless of changes in the value of money. Translation via the monetary/non-monetary method involves monetary assets and monetary liabilities being translated at the closing rate while non-monetary items are translated at their historical rate. Accounting exposure under this method is given by net monetary assets.

In terms of development of accounting reporting, this method of translation foreign subsidiaries' accounts seems to have been a half-way house between the current/non-current method and the all current method.

The temporal method
The temporal method of translation uses the closing rate method for all items stated at replacement cost, realizable value, market value or expected future value, and uses the historical rate for all items stated at historic cost.

The rationale for the temporal approach is that the translation rate used should preserve the accounting principles used to value assets and liabilities in the original financial statements. According to the temporal method the translation rate for each asset or liability depends upon the measurement basis used in the foreign subsidiary's original accounts.

Applied to traditional historic cost accounts, the temporal and monetary/non-monetary methods give almost the same results. The main difference arises in the case of certain items of inventory. Where stock is stated in the original accounts at market value (where it is below historic cost) the temporal method would translate it at the current rate while the monetary/non-monetary approach would use the historic rate of exchange, but it should be emphasized that the temporal method is by no means synonymous with the monetary/non-monetary approach.

Translation exposure – a numerical example

It should be clear that identical firms with identical assets, liabilities, capital structures and trading results may show different translation gains and losses and different translated balance sheets depending upon the method used for converting foreign currency items to home currency values. This can be demonstrated by a simple numerical example.

Assume that a UK company set up a subsidiary in the Netherlands on 1 March and that the opening transactions are booked in the Dutch company's accounts according to the prevailing exchange rate of £1 = NLG3. The opening balance sheet is shown in Table 5.1.

Assume, further, that no additional business or transactions go through the Dutch company during March and consequently the guilder balance sheet at the end of the month remains as at the beginning. But assume that during March sterling fell against the guilder and the exchange rate at the end of the month was £1 = NLG2.5. This means that the sterling-translated balance sheet of the subsidiary will alter, the extent of the change differing according to whether the current/non-current, all current, or monetary/non-monetary method of translation is used. Table 5.1 shows the results.

From the table it will be noted that the translation gain or loss is equal to 16.67 per cent of the accounting exposure. This is, of course, consistent with the movement in sterling value versus the guilder from 3 to 2.5. But it will further be noted from the table that translation outturns range from a gain of over £491,000 to a loss of over £349,000. These differences arise merely because of varying accounting methods.

Translation – moving towards a consensus

Internationally, the accounting profession has been concerned about the position on translation of foreign currency accounting statements. Indeed, the accounting professions in the USA and the UK now have almost identical rules for accounting for foreign currencies in published accounts. Generally speaking, translation of foreign balance sheets uses the current rate method. Transaction gains, whether realized or not, are accounted for through the profit and loss account. But there is a major exception. Where a transaction profit or loss arises from taking on a foreign currency borrowing in a situation in which the borrowing can be designated as a hedge for a net investment denominated in the same foreign currency as the borrowing, then the gain or loss on the borrowing, if it is less than the net investment hedged, would be accounted for by movements in reserves rather than through the income statement. If this kind of transaction gain or loss exceeds the amount of the loss or gain respectively on the net investment hedged, the excess gain or loss is to be reported in the profit and loss account. Non-transaction gains and losses are to be dealt with by reserve accounting direct to the balance sheet rather than through the profit and loss account.

Table 5.1 Example illustrating translation exposure

| | Subsidiary's balance sheet as at 1 March NLG 000 | Subsidiary's balance sheet as at 1 March £000 | Subsidiary's balance sheet as at 31 March translated according to: | | |
			All current rate £000	Current/ non-current £000	Monetary/ non-monetary £000
Fixed assets	8,400	2,800	3,360*	2,800	2,800
Inventory	4,200	1,400	1,680*	1,680*	1,400
Cash	1,065	355	426*	426*	426*
Total assets	13,665	4,555	5,466	4,906	4,626
Current payables	2,100	700	840*	840*	840*
Long-term debt	4,200	1,400	1,680*	1,400	1,680*
Equity	7,365	2,455	2,946	2,666	2,106
Translation gain/(loss)			491	211	(349)
Accounting exposure as at 31 March			2,946	1,266	(2,094)

*Assets and liabilities exposed, as of 31 March, to translation exposure under different translation conventions.

According to the US standard FASB 52, translation of foreign currency revenues and costs (the essence of the income statement) is to be made at the average exchange rate during the accounting period. The British standard SSAP 20 allows the use of either the current rate or the average rate for this purpose. However, it is fair to say that opinion in the UK has moved towards the average rate method.

While translation methods affect group balance sheet values, the key point is that they have nothing to do with economic value. The value of the Dutch subsidiary in the example should not be affected by adopting a different method of accounting. Its worth will be the same whether the all current, current/non-current or monetary/non-monetary method is used. In all probability its discounted net present value will have changed as a result of the strengthened guilder. But this changed present value is hardly what we pick up by using different methods of translating balance sheets. Clearly, changes in value resulting from changed exchange rates shown in terms of different present values. If we are concerned with how true value has changed because of exchange rate movements, we should be looking at economic value and how it changes in sympathy to moving exchange rates. This is what true exposure to exchange rate movements is all about.

Economic exposure

Economic exposure is concerned with the present value of future operating cash flows to be generated by a company's activities and how this present value, expressed in parent currency, changes following exchange rate movements. The concept of economic exposure is most frequently applied to a company's expected operating cash flows from foreign operations, but it can equally well be applied to a firm's home territory operations and the extent to which the present value of those operations alters resultant upon changed exchange rates. For the purpose of convenience, the exposition which follows is based on a firm's foreign operations.

Some experts classify transaction exposure as a subset of economic exposure. They take this view arguing that the present value of an uncovered foreign currency denominated receivable or payable will vary as exchange rates vary. While we accept the logic of this view, in this book we prefer to treat economic and transaction exposures separately. This perspective is adopted because of the different levels of difficulty with which the multinational can monitor and control transaction and economic exposures.

The value of an overseas operation can be expressed as the present value of expected future operating cash flows which are incremental to that overseas activity discounted at the appropriate discount rate. Expressing this present value in terms of the parent currency can be achieved via the formula set out below – but remember that incremental cash flows to the whole group of companies include management fees, royalties and similar kinds of flow as well as direct cash flows from trading operations. The present value of the foreign subsidiary may be expressed as:

$$PV = \sum_{t=0}^{n} \frac{(CI_t - CO_t)e_t}{(1 - r)^t}$$

where PV is the parent currency present value of the foreign business, CI represents estimated future incremental net cash inflows associated with the foreign business expressed in foreign currency, CO is the estimated future incremental net cash outflows associated with the foreign business expressed in foreign currency, e is the expected future exchange rate (expressed in terms of the direct quote in the home territory), r is the appropriate discount rate, namely the rate of return that the parent requires from an investment in the risk class of the overseas business, t is the period for which cash flows are expected and n is the final period for which all flows are expected. The above formulation assumes that all net incremental cash flows accruing to the overseas operation are distributable to the parent company in the home country.

At first sight the reader might conclude that quantifying economic exposure and the impact of changing exchange rates is fairly straight-forward. For example, assume that a British company has a wholly owned French subsidiary with a net present value of FFr120m. If the exchange rate is £1 = FFr8 and it subsequently moves to £1 = FFr10, presumably the value of the subsidiary has moved from £15m to £12m. Such a conclusion would, in all probability, be incorrect. It is necessary to be far more analytical to reach a worthwhile conclusion on valuation.

Devaluation will affect cash inflows and cash outflows as well as affecting the exchange rate. Consider a company competing in export markets. While devaluation will not affect the total market size, it should have a favourable market share effect. The company in the devaluing country should increase sales or profit margins – in short, it should benefit. Similarly, companies competing with imports in the domestic market should also gain since a devaluation will tend to make imported products more expensive in local currency terms. However, this benefit may be offset to some extent by domestic deflation which frequently accompanies devaluation. So, in the import competing sector of the domestic market there will be beneficial and negative impacts. Next, in the purely domestic market, devaluation may lead to reduced company performance in the short term as a result of deflationary measures at home which so often accompany currency depreciation.

All of the above factors affect cash inflows. Devaluations also affect cash outflows. Imported inputs become more expensive. If devaluation is accompanied by domestic deflation it will probably be the case that suppliers' prices will rise as their financing costs move up. An inverse line of reasoning applies with respect to revaluation of a currency.

Getting to grips with economic exposure involves us in analysing the effects of changing exchange rates on the following items:

1. Export sales, where margins and cash flows should change because devaluation should make exports more competitive.

2. Domestic sales, where margins and cash flows should alter substantially in the import competing sector.

3. Pure domestic sales, where margins and cash flows should change in response to deflationary measures which frequently accompany devaluations.

4. Costs of imported inputs, which should rise in response to a devaluation.

5. Cost of domestic inputs, which may vary with exchange rate changes.

The analysis is clearly complex, but it is necessary in order to assess fully how the home currency present value of overseas operations is likely to alter in response to movements in foreign exchange rates.

So far it has been assumed that the parent's present value of its foreign subsidiary is a function of that subsidiary's estimated future net cash flows. In other words, there is an assumption that all cash flows are distributable to the parent. In fact, host governments frequently restrict distribution to foreign parents by exchange controls. Suffice here to say that where distribution of cash flows to the parent is limited, the present value formula needs to be adjusted a little:

$$PV = \sum_{t=0}^{n} \frac{(Div_t + OPF_t)e_t}{(1 + r)^t} + \frac{TVe_n}{(1 + r)^n}$$

The notation is as before except that Div represents the expected net dividend inflow in a particular year, OPF represents other parent flows such as royalties and management fees in a particular period, and TV represents the terminal value remittable over the foreign exchanges at the end of the project's life.

The reader should always bear in mind that economic exposure is equally applicable to the home operations of a firm inasmuch as a change in exchange rates is likely to affect the present value of its home operations; this may arise for all of the reasons which would impinge upon foreign businesses.

There is another, related dimension to economic exposure. A British firm exporting goods to the USA, denominated in dollars, in competition with a German manufacturer will be facing a transaction exposure against the dollar and an economic exposure against the Deutsche Mark. Clearly, as the exchange rate between the pound and the Deutsche Mark changes, so the British manufacturer is in a stronger or weaker position and this will filter through to sales levels, profit and cash generation. As such, the present value of the British company's export business will alter as exchange rates change. Just like the previous kind of economic exposure, this subset is difficult to quantify for reasons similar to those mentioned before.

It can be seen that assessing economic exposure necessarily involves us in a substantial amount of work on elasticities of demand and behaviour of costs in response to changes in exchange rates. But the critical question that we would ask is whether economic exposure (or transaction exposure or translation exposure for that matter) is of any relevance to the financial manager of an international company. This question is addressed in the next chapter.

An overview

Foreign exchange risk arises because the home firm has assets, liabilities, profits or expected future cash flow streams, the value of which (in home currency terms) may alter as a result of exchange rate movements. Changes in exchange rates can change the parent currency value of those assets, liabilities, profits or expected future cash flow streams. Foreign exchange risk falls into one or more of three basic categories: transaction exposure, translation exposure and economic exposure. The first and the last of these are underpinned by expected future cash flows denominated in foreign currencies.

A particular item may be classified under more than one heading. For example, under all translation methods other than the current/non-current method, a long-term foreign denominated borrowing is certainly both a transaction exposure (because the home currency equivalent to repay the loan varies as exchange rates change) and a translation exposure.

The relevance of classifying foreign exchange risk according to the three types discussed in this chapter is that we would advocate that some categories of exposure should be actively managed by the headquarters treasury while our prescription for other categories is that, since they do not matter, there is little point in applying treasury time in taking action to avoid the risk. These topics are taken up in the next chapter.

6

Why worry about foreign exchange risk?

Most of the arguments about whether or not foreign exchange risk matters draw on material summarized in the earlier chapters. Foreign exchange exposure can be looked at from three separate perspectives: transaction exposure, economic exposure and translation exposure. The previous chapter provided a discussion on these. In this chapter we consider the extent to which each should be a relevant factor in terms of the financial objective of maximization of the value of the firm.

Transaction exposure

Transaction exposure is concerned with how changes in exchange rates affect the value of anticipated foreign currency denominated cash flows relating to transactions already entered into. According to much, although by no means all, of the empirical work on the expectations theory part of the four-way equivalence model, the current forward rate is an unbiased predictor of the future spot rate. In the long term, using the forward rate to approximate the future spot rate results in being on the high side as often as on the low side – which is what the term 'unbiased predictor' means.

It follows that covering forward will, in the long run, be of little worth to the firm that has a large number of foreign currency denominated transactions. It might as well not cover forward but take the spot rate at the time the payable or receivable matures since the results from adopting the strategy of covering forward will, eventually, equal the results achieved from running the debt to maturity and taking the spot rate. Indeed, given that foreign exchange dealers charge their customers a wider bid/offer spread on forward contracts compared with spot transactions, it follows that avoiding cover should be more profitable in the long run.

But it can also be an extremely dangerous policy. By failing to cover transaction exposure, a firm may incur a vast loss on a single very large receivable or payable denominated in a foreign currency. This may result in an overall loss for the firm in a particular financial period which could, in its turn, lead to financial distress. It is not much comfort to the finance director of a company which has just failed as a direct result of not covering transaction exposure that it would have been all right in the long run because at some time in the future it could hope to win on another contract the amount that it has just lost on this one. There is little consolation in the company being all right in the long run if it is dead in the short run. Bearing this in mind, the prudent finance director will argue that covering forward reduces potential variability in home currency cash flows as well as in profits. Thus covering forward reduces some of the threat of short-term financial problems. In the longer run, the cost of such insurance against foreign exchange risk is small since it in effect amounts to the dealer's spread on forward transactions less the spread on spot deals. It may not be the case that this policy maximizes profits in the long run, but from the standpoint of a risk-averse manager it has clear appeal.

It is understandable that the firm which enters into few foreign currency denominated transactions may cover all of them. It is also understandable that risk-averse managers in companies with a vast number of foreign currency denominated transactions would make a habit of covering them. However, many treasurers in such firms adopt policies of selective covering.

The same kind of argument, but with some essential differences, applies with respect to lending and borrowing denominated in foreign currencies. Most lending or borrowing involves respective receipt or payment of interest at regular intervals with capital repayment at a specified date. According to the international Fisher effect, the penalty for borrowing in a hard currency will be exactly offset by the benefit of a low interest rate. This can best be illustrated by an example. Assume that expected inflation in the UK is higher than that in Switzerland. If we begin from a base year in which exchange rates between sterling and the Swiss franc are in equilibrium, then we would anticipate, via purchasing power parity, that the Swiss franc would strengthen against sterling; and, via the Fisher effect, we would expect interest rates in Switzerland to be lower than sterling interest rates. Thus the international Fisher effect would be suggesting a weakening of sterling against the Swiss franc compensated for by lower Swiss franc interest rates. So a company considering raising £5m might do so in sterling and it might expect then to pay a higher interest rate than would be the case were that same company to raise the money in Swiss francs. But raising the money in Swiss francs would have the drawback that when repayment was due the company would probably have to find in excess of £5m sterling because of the strengthening of the

Swiss franc during the period that the loan was outstanding. Leaving aside imperfections in the market created by taxation treatment of foreign exchange losses on loans (although in the real world these market imperfections created by non-symmetrical tax treatment are far too important to be left aside), the international Fisher effect would predict that the gain resulting from the lower interest rate on the Swiss franc borrowing would be exactly offset by the loss on capital repayment at maturity.

The above kind of situation is illustrative of how the international Fisher effect underpins the argument that foreign exchange exposure on borrowings does not matter. In the real world, though, while some studies suggest that the international Fisher effect holds in the medium to long term, others suggest that we can wait an awfully long time for it to assert itself. For the international company, these findings are crucial. In the long run our company borrowing in hard currencies might expect to come out even and thus be indifferent (before tax but not after tax) about the currency denomination of its borrowings, but in the short run its Swiss borrowing might wipe it out.

This kind of problem has dramatically affected more than a few British companies. Laker Airways arranged lease finance denominated in US dollars for the bulk of its aircraft at a time when the dollar was strengthening; and J. Lyons had a wealth of Swiss franc borrowings on its balance sheet at a time when sterling was weak against the Swiss franc. Laker went out of business partly, but by no means solely, because of its dollar borrowings; Lyons was rescued when it was taken over by Allied Breweries but its plight was largely a result of its uncovered hard currency debt.

The problem that treasurers of international companies have is not just that the international Fisher effect is found empirically to be a long-run phenomenon but that when they undertake a foreign currency denominated borrowing the exchange rates between the home currency and the foreign one may not be in equilibrium. Subsequent correction of the disequilibrium can incur a vast loss (or profit) for the international borrower.

Perhaps it is fair to conclude that were the four-way equivalence model to hold in the real world immutably and with no time lags, and if the tax treatment on currency losses and gains on repayment of foreign denominated loans were on the same footing as interest paid and received, then transaction exposure would not matter. But the real world is not so convenient. The four-way equivalence model does involve time lags – and very big ones. Tax treatment of interest and currency gains and losses are not symmetrical. All of this means that transaction exposure is important to international financial executives. In short, it needs to be managed.

Economic exposure

Economic exposure refers to the possibility that the present value of future operating cash flows of a business, expressed in parent currency, may be affected by a change in foreign exchange rates. According to purchasing power parity theory, exchange rate changes are associated with different relative rates of inflation. The argument that economic exposure does not matter draws on the purchasing power parity theory.

Devaluation of the home currency tends to favour companies competing in export markets. It also has a favourable impact in import-competing areas, as well as creating advantages for firms that are domestically sourced (imports become relatively more expensive) and domestically financed. Revaluations have inversely opposite effects.

A relatively high domestic inflation rate, if not accompanied by devaluation, has an adverse effect on companies competing in export markets and those competing domestically with imported goods. It adversely affects firms which are domestically sourced and (because the tendency will be for the home interest rate to rise) domestically financed.

Devaluation creates advantages which correct disadvantages flowing from high relative inflation rates. The benefits created for some firms by devaluation should offset earlier adverse effects created by inflation. If relative inflation rates are being accompanied by appropriate exchange rate adjustments, as predicted by purchasing power parity, it may be argued that we have a situation where the overall effect is neutral. The benefits of devaluation exactly offset the earlier penalties of inflation.

But should this be universally true? Maybe the above argument would be applicable to the firm all of whose costs were inflating at the same rate as the general level of inflation in the country in which it was based. The devaluation or revaluation would be exactly offsetting movements in the firm's specific costs. In these circumstances economic exposure would not matter to the firm.

Of course, it is unusual for the firm's individual costs to move in line with general inflation. And where they do not, economic exposure will matter to the firm. Indeed, multinationals consider relocating or switching manufacture from one country to another to correct for local costs having inflated in excess of general inflation levels or, more specifically, in excess of competitor nations' costs.

If, then, economic exposure does matter to the international company, should it endeavour to hedge this exposure through forward market purchases or sales of currency? It is believed that the answer to this question veers towards the negative. This conclusion has been reached not because economic exposure is based on uncertain cash flows nor because it is difficult to quantify since it involves detailed analysis of elasticities of demand. Instead it is believed that there are easier ways to deal with the fact that the present value of expected cash flows accruing from operations may alter in response to changes in exchange rates. This simple way involves financing operations, either partially or wholly, in the foreign currency (or currencies) which is judged as having a significant impact upon the present value of operations. It should be mentioned that this approach does not provide an exact cover for economic exposure because the hedge via financing is a function of relative inflation rates with differences corrected via purchasing power parity; the changing value of operating cash flows is affected by relative price movements and cost changes of specific goods sold and costs incurred, and these are only partially corrected by changing exchange rates based on general inflation levels.

Anecdotal evidence has been encountered of international companies actively managing economic exposure via forward markets and currency options. This involves the calculation of exposed net present values of operating cash flows, deducting from them the hedge effect achieved by financing and then using forward and/or option markets to hedge net exposure should this be deemed to be advantageous. How forwards and options work are dealt with in subsequent chapters.

There is a strong case for monitoring and managing economic exposure by entering into forward or option markets to protect the present value of expected future cash flows where the period of the firm's involvement in a particular overseas environment has a finite time horizon, such as a joint venture that will terminate after three years of operation. Since the firm's involvement does not span sufficient time to ensure a cycle running through to equilibrium, economic exposure can be material. However, this kind of situation has more of a transaction exposure dimension since the residual value of the project will, presumably, be remitted to headquarters at the end of the period of overseas involvement.

Translation exposure

Translation exposure arises as a result of the process of consolidation of foreign currency items into group financial statements denominated in the currency of the parent company. Some items frequently viewed as being solely translation exposure are essentially transaction exposure items. This is the case with respect to foreign currency denominated borrowings or lendings. Repayment of the loan requires cash to pass from borrower to lender, and this creates a cash flow exposure. With respect to the question of whether foreign exchange exposure matters for these kinds of item which may be classified as both transaction exposure and translation exposure, the answer should flow from viewing them as transaction rather than as translation items.

Different translation methods may have different impacts upon a firm's reported earnings per share. But do these different accounting methods affect the valuation of the firm? Clearly, from a theoretical standpoint the accounting methods of reporting for overseas subsidiaries' results should not on their own have an impact upon valuation of a subsidiary. Their valuation to the parent company should be a function of expected future cash flows which are distributable to the parent. Admittedly, this may alter as exchange rates alter. We would argue theoretically that subsidiaries' values change in response to movements in exchange rates because their present value, in home currency terms, is perceived by investors to have altered. Note that this theoretical argument has nothing to do with accounting reporting for foreign operations.

But the key question is how does the investment community interpret changing subsidiary results based on changed translation methods? Such a question is entirely empirical – it is concerned with how the real world judges things. Our answer therefore draws on real world investigations.

Under FASB 8 (the now defunct USA accounting standard) translation gains and losses were included in the group consolidated profit and loss account and caused wide fluctuations in reported corporate profits and earnings per share. It is often stated that managing directors and finance directors love to see a smooth progression to earnings per share and it is frequently asserted that such growth is near to the security analyst's heart too. This view has undoubtedly led to some questionable decisions by multinational companies designed to hedge translation exposure by incurring transaction exposure.

The international giant ITT is reported as having sold forward $600m worth of foreign currencies with a view partially to hedging balance sheet exposure. The dollar fell relative to most foreign currencies and this resulted in a translation gain and an offsetting loss on forward cover. This gain was unrealized but the forward loss involved a cash loss in the order of $48m. ITT achieved its objective of partially hedging balance sheet exposure. It is worth mentioning that ITT was by no means alone in its response to accounting exposure under FASB 8. A number of studies reported similar actions by US-based multinationals designed to counter translation exposure by incurring transaction exposure. But many would argue that such transactions make little or no economic sense. FASB 52 (the US accounting standard which replaced FASB 8) obviates the need for any company to take this illogical action. This newer accounting standard essentially puts all translation gains and losses direct to reserves on the balance sheet rather than via the profit and loss account. This is similar to present accounting rules in Britain.

Did the reporting requirements of FASB 8 affect the stock market performance of companies reporting translation gains and losses? Again, this is entirely an empirical question. The most notable study in this area was undertaken in the USA by Roland Dukes. He set out to investigate the stock market effect of FASB 8 reporting requirements. He compared the stock market performance of a sample of over 450 multinational companies with a control sample of domestic firms. The empirical results are that the security returns behaviour of portfolios of multinational firms, despite the impact of FASB 8 upon reported earnings, is not significantly different from the return behaviour of comparable portfolios of domestic firms. His conclusions are that the US stock market is not fooled by pure translation gains and losses. Moreover, the actions of some multinationals in hedging translation exposure by entering into forward contracts is seen not only to be illogical from a deductive standpoint but also to be unjustified empirically since stock market analysts seem not to be interested in pure translation gains and losses. In short, the available evidence accords with the theoretical view that pure translation exposure does not matter.

Firms frequently consider hedging forecast foreign-denominated profit earned by subsidiaries. Although this may be viewed as a translation exposure, it really has more substantial elements of transaction or economic exposure. This is because the dividend remitted to the home territory headquarters is a function of profit. According to this view there is a case for hedging future foreign currency profit – but as an economic exposure rather than as a translation exposure.

An overview

Transaction exposure is concerned with how changes in exchange rates affect the value of anticipated foreign currency denominated cash flows relating to transactions already entered into. Empirically it is frequently found that the forward rate is an unbiased predictor of the future spot rate. This means that failing to take cover should yield similar results in the long run to hedging. However, failing to cover may have disastrous short-term results. Avoiding these potential financial pitfalls by selective covering is therefore a logical strategy. It is little compensation to the uncovered firm that has just gone bust to argue that it would have been all right in the long run.

Economic exposure relates to the possibility that the present value of future cash flows of a firm may be affected by foreign currency movements.

But exchange rate changes are related, via purchasing power parity, to differences in relative inflation rates. The firm whose foreign operation experiences cost inflation exactly in line with general inflation should be returned to its original value by changes in the exchange rate exactly in line with purchasing power parity. In these circumstances, economic exposure may be argued not to matter. Most firms, though, experience specific cost inflations which differ from general inflation. In this situation economic exposure does matter. Our recommended approach to minimizing this kind of exposure is to finance operations in the currency to which the firm's value is sensitive.

Translation exposure arises as a result of the process of consolidation of foreign currency denominated items into group financial statements produced in the currency of the parent company. Research work has tended to indicate that pure translation exposure does not affect share prices. As such, it seems that translation exposure should not matter and it is consequently recommended that pure translation exposures need not be covered.

7

Internal techniques of managing foreign exchange exposure

There is a wide range of methods available to minimize foreign exchange risk. This chapter and the next focus respectively upon internal and external techniques. Internal methods use tools of exposure management which are part of a firm's own financial management within the group of companies concerned and do not resort to special contractual relationships with third parties outside the firm. External techniques use contractual means to insure against potential foreign exchange losses.

Internal techniques embrace netting, matching, leading and lagging, pricing policies and asset/liability management. Some of these may be constrained by local exchange controls – netting, matching and leading and lagging are illegal in some countries and restricted in others. External techniques include forward contracts, borrowing, discounting, factoring, government exchange risk guarantees and currency options. It should be borne in mind that, for many less developed countries, there is no forward market in their currencies.

Netting

Netting involves associated companies which trade with each other. The technique is simple. Group companies merely settle interaffiliate indebtedness for the net amount owing. Gross intragroup trade receivables and payables are netted out. The simplest scheme is known as bilateral netting and simply involves pairs of companies. Each pair of associates nets out their own individual positions with each other and cash flows are reduced by the lower of each company's purchases from or sales to its netting partner. Bilateral netting involves no attempt to bring in the net positions of other group companies.

Netting basically reduces the number of intercompany payments and receipts which pass over the foreign exchanges. Fairly straightforward to operate, the main practical problem in bilateral netting is usually the decision about what currency to use for settlement.

Multilateral netting is more complicated but in principle no different from bilateral netting. Multilateral netting involves more than two associated companies' indebtedness and virtually always involves the services of the group treasury. Bilateral netting involves only two sides and is usually undertaken without the involvement of the corporate centre.

Multilateral netting yields considerable savings in exchange and transfer costs but it requires a centralized communications system and discipline on the part of subsidiary companies. It should be noted that many countries' exchange controls put restrictions on bilateral and multilateral netting. Exchange control regulations need to be investigated carefully before embarking on a policy of netting.

Netting reduces banking costs and increases central control of intercompany settlements. The reduced number and amount of payments yield savings in terms of buy/sell spreads in the spot and forward markets and reduced bank charges. It is difficult to estimate total benefits but as a guide to the extent of gains flowing from netting techniques, it has been estimated that savings of approximately ⅙ per cent of the flows are eliminated.

Matching

Although netting and matching are terms which are frequently used interchangeably, there are distinctions. Strictly speaking, netting is a term applied to potential flows within a group of companies whereas matching can be applied to both intragroup and to third-party balancing.

Matching is a mechanism whereby a company matches its foreign currency inflows with its foreign currency outflows in respect of amount and approximate timing. Receipts in a particular currency are used to make payments in that currency thereby reducing the need for a group of companies to go through the foreign exchange markets to the unmatched portion of foreign currency cash flows.

The prerequisite for a matching operation is a two-way cash flow in the same foreign currency within a group of companies; this gives rise to a potential for natural matching. This should be distinguished from parallel matching, in which the matching is achieved with receipt and payment in different currencies but these currencies are expected to move closely together, near enough in parallel. An example is the EMS currencies (see Chapter 14). Of course, there is always the chance with parallel matching that the currencies concerned may move away from their previously parallel paths, for example a realignment within the EMS. In this case the expected match fails to be realized.

The practical mechanics of matching is rather like multilateral netting since it involves the group treasury and gives rise to the need for information centralization with the group finance function just before settlement. Practical problems may arise because of the uncertain timing of third-party receipts and payments. Unexpected delays can create problems for the multinational treasury in its endeavours to match receipts and payments. The possibility that receipt of a sum due on a certain settlement day is postponed but payment is nonetheless made on that same date as originally anticipated, creates obvious difficulties.

For this reason, success in matching is a function of the quality of information coming to the corporate financial centre, including realistic and accurate predictions of settlement dates. Like netting, the extent of matching is constrained by the exchange controls of some countries.

Leading and lagging

Leading and lagging refers to the adjustment of credit terms between companies. It is most usually applied with respect to payments between associate companies within a group. Leading means paying an obligation in advance of the due date; lagging means delaying payment of an obligation beyond its due date. Leading and lagging are foreign exchange management tactics designed to take advantage of expected devaluations and revaluations of currencies.

An example may help to indicate the processes involved. Suppose that subsidiary b in country B owes money to subsidiary a in country A with payment due in three months' time and with the debt denominated in US dollars. Suppose further that country B's currency is expected to devalue within three months relative to the US dollar and also *vis-à-vis* country A's currency. Obviously if company b leads (that is, if it pays early) it will have to part with less of country B's currency to buy US dollars to make payment to company a. So the temptation to lead is attractive.

However, it is necessary to look a little further than this. Should the international Fisher effect be holding in the short term, then the interest rate on deposits in country B's currency should exceed the interest rate on US dollar deposits by the amount of the expected devaluation. Decisions on leading and lagging need to take account of relative interest rates as well as expected currency movements. There is a third relevant dimension too, namely the effective tax rates on interest in differing countries. So reverting to our example, we need to compare the net of tax cash flow effects after allowing for interest from a group standpoint. Thus should company *b* lead, it will save in terms of country B's currency by beating the impending devaluation. But the group will then receive a US dollar interest rate rather than an interest rate based on the currency of country B – and this US dollar interest rate should be lower than that of country B's currency. All of this has to be taken into account on a net of tax basis over the period of the lead.

A similar example could be devised which would suggest lagging. Should country B's currency be expected to revalue or harden against the US dollar, then lagging would, on the face of things, be the preferred tactic. But once again, as is always the case with leading and lagging decisions, we need to consider from a group standpoint the combined impacts of:

1. The expected currency change and its timing.
2. Relative interest rates.
3. After-tax effects.

As with matching, the group treasury is usually involved to ensure that the timing of intercompany settlement is functional from a group standpoint rather than merely from a local one. It is also worth mentioning that performance measurement may be affected if some subsidiaries are asked to lead and some to lag. Clearly, the subsidiary which does the leading loses interest receivable and incurs interest charges on the funds led. To overcome this problem, evaluation of performance is frequently done on a pre-interest, pre-tax basis.

The existence of local minority interests gives rise to complications on leading and lagging decisions. Significant local shareholders in the paying subsidiary always raise strong objections because of the added interest costs and lower profitability resulting from the consequent local borrowing. In such cases the interests of the minority shareholders appear to be subordinated to those of the majority shareholder, the parent company. The existence of strong local minorities frequently results in companies refraining from lead and lag techniques.

Leading and lagging may also be constrained by exchange control regulations. Leading and lagging affect balance of payments figures as well as exchange rates. Because of this, host governments frequently impose allowable bands on credit terms which must be followed in all international trading.

The application of leading and lagging techniques extends beyond the realm of pure risk minimization in exposure management. Opportunities are created for taking aggressive stances on financing. It should be understood that this strategy is based upon the view, borne out by empirical evidence, that the international Fisher effect does not hold in the short term. Thus an expected devaluation in a host country would probably cause an international company to consider raising local finance to repay foreign currency denominated borrowings.

Price variation

Price variation involves increasing selling prices to counter the adverse effects of exchange rate changes. This tactic raises the question as to why the company has not already raised prices if it is able to do so. In some countries, price increases are the only legally available tactic of exposure management. In most South American countries this is true; most other methods are illegal, there is no forward market and local financial markets are so shallow as to make borrowings with the objectives of achieving exposure management impossible.

We now turn to price variation on intercompany trade. Transfer pricing is the term used to refer to the pricing of goods and services which change hands within a group of companies. As an exposure management technique, transfer price variation refers to the arbitrary pricing of intercompany sales of goods and services at a higher or lower price than the fair, arm's length price. This fair price will be the market price if there is an existing market or, if there is not, the price which would be charged to a third-party customer. Taxation authorities, customs and excise departments and exchange control regulations in most countries require that arm's length pricing be used and in virtually all countries in the world tax authorities have the power to impute a price where transfer price manipulation is suspected and customs and excise departments base excise duty on an imputed price when the transfer price is considered to be unfair. Nonetheless many multinationals attempt to maximize after-tax group cash flows by transfer pricing in order to minimize tax payable and move funds around the world.

Invoicing in foreign currency

Companies engaged in exporting and importing, whether of goods or services, are concerned with decisions relating to the currency in which goods and services are invoiced. Trading in a foreign currency gives rise to transaction exposure with its attendant risks and opportunities. Although trading purely in a company's home currency has the advantage of simplicity, it fails to take account of the fact that the currency in which goods are invoiced has become an essential aspect of the overall marketing package given to the customer.

Sellers will usually wish to sell in their own currency or the currency in which they incur cost. This avoids foreign exchange exposure. But buyers' preferences may be for other currencies. Many markets, such as oil or aluminium, in effect require that sales be made in the same currency as that quoted by major competitors, which may not be the seller's own currency. In a buyer's market, sellers tend increasingly to invoice in the buyer's ideal currency. The closer the seller can approximate the buyer's aims, the greater chance he or she has to make the sale.

Should the seller elect to invoice in foreign currency, perhaps because the prospective customer prefers it that way or because sellers tend to follow the market leader, then the seller should choose only a major currency in which there is an active forward market for maturities at least as long as the payment period. Currencies which are of limited convertibility, chronically weak or with only a limited forward market should not be considered.

Where there is the prospect of a major export to a country with a small economy, such that the value of the contract is likely to be a significant factor in that country's balance of payments, then further considerations apply. The seller is advised to avoid the buyer's currency. Where the government itself or one of its agencies is the customer, it behoves the seller to bear in mind that the customer is able to devalue the currency prior to payment, effectively reducing proceeds in the currency of the exporter.

The seller's ideal currency is either his or her own, or one which is stable relative to it, but often the seller is forced to choose the market leader's currency. Whatever the chosen currency, it should certainly be one with a deep forward market. For the buyer, though, the ideal currency is usually its own or one that is stable relative to it, or it may be a currency of which the purchaser has reserves.

Strong buyers may be in a position to insist on their own currency being used for pricing. It is often a condition of any tender or deal, and quotes in other currencies are simply ignored. An advantage to the seller when selling in the purchaser's home currency is that payment is rendered simpler for the buyer. In these circumstances payment is usually much more rapid, and this may constitute a good reason for invoicing in the buyer's currency.

Of course, many international traders seek to buy in the same currencies as those in which they receive income, in order to net out exposure at source. This will not necessarily be their home currency. Furthermore, many markets are economically structured in such a way that competitors follow the market leader. In such circumstances it is often the practice of participants to quote in the same currency as that in which the market leader quotes – and this may be the home currency of neither the buyer nor of the seller.

Occasionally the invoice currency becomes a bone of contention between seller and buyer. Often a proxy currency, namely one that moves similarly to the buyer's currency, is resorted to as a way of resolving the impasse. Another technique, which was popular in the past although it is less frequently used now, is the use of a currency clause whereby payment is made in one currency but the amount due is fixed by reference to another.

Usually in export contracts at least one party enters into a foreign exchange transaction. It may be the exporter if he is selling in a foreign currency; it may be the importer if he is buying in a currency other than his own. If the currency of the contract is not the home currency of either the importer or the exporter, then both will have to undertake a foreign exchange transaction. Given this background, it is eminently sensible to arrange matters such that the cost of completing the foreign exchange contract should be minimized. Foreign currency markets within Europe vary widely in their competitiveness and spread or commission structure. For example, in some Scandinavian countries, exchange controls require that a local company does its foreign exchange transactions with a bank in the home country, where costs are high by London standards. For those who are able to access it, the London market is the world's cheapest foreign exchange market to deal in. Where one of the parties to a trade is based in a country where exchange controls make it relatively expensive to use local foreign exchange markets it may be wise to structure the deal such that the London market may be accessed. This is pertinent for intergroup trading. For an Anglo-Scandinavian trade it may be worthwhile to invoice in the Scandinavian currency so that no foreign exchange transaction arises in Scandinavia and it will be in London where the foreign exchange deal takes place.

The arguments set out above all relate to marketing aspects of the question of invoicing in foreign currency. None relates to aspects such as seeking to invoice in strong currencies, something which seems to concern a great number of companies. Our view is that in countries without exchange controls, time spent seeking to invoice in strong currencies is time wasted since if the company wishes to be long in particular currencies it is free to buy these whether or not there is any underlying trade. Forward markets, futures and currency options all provide scope for the aggressive company to take positions in currencies if its senior management so desires. This would seem to be a more direct method of backing one's judgement on currencies without involving directly the basic business operations of the company.

Having said this, there are commercial reasons why a company in a country with or without exchange controls might prefer to use a strong currency as the medium in which it invoices in international trade. The most frequently quoted reason is to enable the firm to maintain stable price lists in circumstances where new price lists are expensive to alter. In countries with exchange controls it is usually the case that trade represents the only mechanism by which a company is legally able to take positions in foreign currencies.

Many companies with strong positions in markets where they are under short-term pressure from competitors may decide to invoice in a currency expected to be weak. Thus as the currency of invoicing depreciates, so the customer receives an increasing discount on the goods without the company formally announcing a price cut. This tactic enables the company to protect market share while market conditions are poor. Conversely, a company in a strong market position in a seller's market might, in the short term, specify a strong currency for invoicing thus obtaining the benefit of a continuously rising price in home currency without formally changing its prices.

In countries where exchange controls limit the taking of positions in foreign currencies, international companies use cross-frontier trade as one of the few mechanisms available to back their commercial judgement on future exchange rate movements. In these circumstances, and with respect to third-party trade, the defensive strategy is to attempt to invoice all exports and have all imports invoiced in the home currency irrespective of the strength and weakness of other currencies. By contrast, the aggressive tactic is to seek to invoice export sales in hard currencies and seek to obtain purchases invoiced in relatively soft currencies. When exchange controls are in place and forward markets are expensive to use, the currency of invoicing technique becomes pertinent. Customers frequently seek to buy goods in weak currencies while the selling company may prefer to invoice in strong currencies. So there is a clear conflict of interests. Marketing executives may prefer to close a sale by whatever means possible and may be functionally influenced to choose the weak currency while this policy is dysfunctional from a total company standpoint. Evidently there should be some marketing systems control mechanism which prevents this dysfunctional tactic.

We now turn to currency of invoicing in the context of intercompany trade. Analysed from a pre-tax point of view, the distinction between aggressive and defensive currency of invoicing disappears when looking at intercompany trade between subsidiaries of equal ownership status – but this is not so where there are minority interests. Currency of invoicing is a zero sum game and therefore the potential benefit to one subsidiary from currency of invoicing equals the potential loss to the other. However, after-tax effects must never be left out of our decision-making criteria, and in this context there may be gains to be achieved from currency of invoicing techniques. Consider two subsidiaries, A and B (both in different countries), which trade with each other. Suppose that A pays a higher marginal tax rate than B. In these circumstances, and with all other things being equal, A might logically invoice B in a weak currency while B invoices A in a strong currency. This policy concentrates exchange profits in B and puts losses into A hence increasing overall after-tax income and cash flow.

Asset and liability management

We now consider the final internal technique of exposure management; this is known as asset and liability management. This technique can be used to manage balance sheet, income statement or cash flow exposures. As stated earlier, we believe that concentration on cash flow exposure makes economic sense but emphasis on pure translation exposure is misplaced. Hence our focus here is on asset/liability management as a cash flow exposure management technique.

In essence, asset/liability management can involve aggressive or defensive postures. In the aggressive attitude, the firm simply increases exposed cash inflows denominated in currencies expected to be strong or increases exposed cash outflows denominated in weak currencies. By contrast, the defensive approach involves matching cash inflows and outflows according to their currency of denomination, irrespective of whether they are in strong or weak currencies.

Commentators frequently distinguish between operating variables and financing variables. Consider operating variables first. Suppose that a UK exporter with an ongoing inflow from sales in Deutsche Marks wishes to avoid the mark exposure; he will most probably use the forward market to do this. However, he might decide to source a significant volume of purchases from Germany, such purchases being denominated in Deutsche Marks. By adopting this policy there is a partial match of currency denomination of inflow with currency denomination of outflow.

With respect to financing variables, the international company has considerable discretion in terms of asset/liability management. The aggressive stance will be to increase exposed cash, debtors and loans receivable in strong currencies (duly taking consideration of interest impact, currency movements and tax effects) and increase borrowings and trade creditors in weak currencies (again allowing for interest effects, currency depreciation and tax impacts). At the same time, policy will involve reducing exposed borrowings and trade creditors in strong currencies and reducing cash, debtors and loans receivable in weak currencies. In the multinational company operating in a weak currency country, the aim will be to acquire local debt and remit cash balances as quickly as possible to the hard currency parent either as dividend remittances or as parent loan repayments. The capital structure of subsidiaries based in weak currency countries may be organized to facilitate transfer of funds. For example, retained earnings may not be capitalized so that dividend flexibility is maintained by keeping up revenue reserves. Also, a high ratio of intercompany debt to parent equity in the subsidiary company's capital structure might help the repatriation of money in circumstances where a high dividend payment might be restricted or discriminated against.

However, some of these financial strategies are constrained in many countries by a paucity of local financial sources. Furthermore, host governments often impose limits for debt to equity ratios and restrict dividend repatriation to certain percentages of capital raised outside of the host country. Host governments frequently also penalize, with heavy taxes, dividends in excess of certain stipulated levels.

An overview

Internal techniques of foreign exchange exposure management are methods which do not resort to special contractual relationships outside the group of companies concerned. Internal techniques embrace netting, matching, leading and lagging, pricing policies and asset/liability management.

8

External techniques of managing foreign exchange exposure

External techniques of exposure management resort to contractual relationships outside of a group of companies in order to reduce the risk of foreign exchange losses. External techniques include forward exchange contracts, short-term borrowing, financial futures contracts, currency options, discounting bills receivable, factoring receivables, currency overdrafts, currency swaps and government exchange risk guarantees. Each of these, bar currency swaps, financial futures and currency options, is briefly considered in this chapter.

Forward markets

Forward markets are available in most, but not all, major currencies of the world. Although in some markets very large sums may be difficult to deal, forward markets for periods out to ten years are available for popular currencies such as the US dollar against sterling, Deutsche Marks, Swiss francs, yen, guilders, French francs, Canadian dollars, ECUs and so on. Generally speaking, the larger the deal, the longer the settlement date is away and the more exotic the currencies involved, the less is the likelihood that a forward contract is obtainable.

A forward foreign exchange contract is an agreement between two parties to exchange one currency for another at some future date. The rate at which the exchange is to be made, the delivery date, and the amounts involved are fixed at the time of the agreement. Such a contract must be distinguished from a foreign exchange futures contract, so a brief definition is given here. A futures foreign exchange contract is a contract between two parties for the exchange of a standardized amount of foreign currency at a standard future date. In both the London International Financial Futures Exchange and the Chicago International Money Market the sterling/US dollar contract is for £25,000 with delivery dates in both markets fixed for the second Wednesday of the contract month which may be either March, June, September or December. A forward contract is usually completed by actual delivery of the currency involved. Futures contracts are more usually closed out by completing a deal in the reverse direction before the maturity date – rather than actually taking delivery on the delivery date.

Reference was made in Chapter 3 to the methods by which bankers quote forward rates. Maybe it is worth while briefly revising the content of that chapter, if this is not already at the reader's fingertips.

Trading purpose of the forward market

By entering into a forward foreign exchange contract, a UK importer or exporter is able to fix, at the time of the contract, a price for the purchase or sale of a fixed amount of foreign currency for delivery and payment at a specified future time. By so doing they may eliminate foreign exchange risk through future exchange rate fluctuations. This enables the exact sterling value of an international commercial contract to be calculated despite the fact that payment is to be made in the future in a foreign currency. Figure 8.1 indicates the mechanism of forward cover.

If a foreign currency stands at premium in the forward market, it shows that the currency is 'stronger' than the home currency in that forward market. By contrast, if a foreign currency stands at a discount in the forward market, it shows that the currency is 'weaker' than the home currency in that forward market. The words stronger and weaker are put in inverted commas because, in the context of forward markets, strength and weakness merely take account of interest rate differentials as suggested by interest rate parity.

Of course, the reality of the business world is such that one cannot be certain when a customer will pay a bill. He may pay before the due date or he may pay afterwards. In the example in Figure 8.1 it was assumed that the French customer would pay on 31 July 1995, that is three months after invoice date. Let us suppose now that the French purchaser is expected to pay on some uncertain date between 30 June and 31 August 1995.

Forward options

The British exporter may decide to cover despite an uncertain payment date via a forward option. How does the forward option work? Like all forward

Contract data

Seller	UK exporter
Buyer	French importer
Contract date	1 May 1995
Credit term	3 months
Expected payment date	31 July 1995
Invoice value	FFr 5m

Exchange rates quotes at 1 May 1995

Spot	7.92¾–7.93½
2 months forward	3⅛–3½ cpm
3 months forward	9⅝–8⅞ cpm
4 months forward	12½–11⅝

Outright exchange rate quotes at 1 May 1995

Spot	7.92¾–7.93½
1 month forward	7.88⅞–7.90
2 months forward	7.86–7.87⅜
3 months forward	7.83⅛–7.84⅝
4 months forward	7.80¼–7.81⅞

Mechanism of forward contract

1 May 1995	UK exporter sells FFr 5m forward 3 months at 7.84⅝
31 July 1995	UK exporter receives FFr 5m from French importer
	UK exporter delivers FFr 5m and receives sterling at the rate of FFr 7.84⅝ equals £1
	For FFr 5m he receives £637,755

Figure 8.1 Forward cover example.

contracts, the exchange rate is irrevocably fixed when the contract is made, but with a forward option contract the precise maturity date is left open – it is for the company to decide subsequently. There is a caveat, though; the maturity date must fall within a specified option period. Reverting to our numerical example, assume that the UK exporter expects payment between 30 June and 31 August 1995 – that is between two and four months from invoice date. Since the bank giving the option as to timing does not know exactly when exercise of the option will occur, it charges the premium or discount for the most costly of the settlement dates within the customer's option period. In other words, the bank charges its customer the worst rate during the option period. In our example, the forward option is over the third and fourth months. In Figure 8.1 it will be seen that the rate is therefore FFr7.87⅜; in this case (but not always) the rate to the seller of francs is the full two months' discount. This is the worst rate between month two and month four for selling French francs.

It should be clearly understood that the forward option contract, or optional date forward contract as it is sometimes called, is not a currency option. The forward option is optional in terms of the date of delivery – currency must be delivered under the contract. However, under a currency option, currency need not be delivered.

Swap deals

Another method of dealing with unspecified settlement dates is by a swap deal. This method is virtually always cheaper than covering by way of forward options. A swap involves the simultaneous buying and selling of a currency for different maturities. Swap deals used for forward cover are of two basic types: forward/forward and spot/forward. In either case, the exporter begins by covering the foreign currency transaction forward to an arbitrarily selected but fixed date, just as in an ordinary fixed-date forward contract. Then, if the precise settlement date is subsequently agreed before the initial forward contract matures, the original settlement date may be extended to the exact date by a forward/forward swap. Alternatively, if an exact settlement date is not agreed by the date when the initial forward contract matures, the forward cover may be extended by a spot/forward swap. This may sound quite complicated; a closer look shows that it is not all that difficult.

A forward/forward swap, or forward swap as it is sometimes called, is merely a pair of forward exchange contracts involving a forward purchase and a forward sale of a currency, simultaneously entered into but for different maturities. A numerical example may help describe how the forward/forward swap works.

Assume that the details of an export contract from Britain to France are as set out in Figure 8.1 except that the expected settlement date is uncertain (maybe because delivery date is equally uncertain). The British exporter takes out a forward contract on 1 May 1995 (the date of the sale contract with the French importer). This forward contract is for an arbitrary period, say two months. So he sells FFr5m forward for delivery on 30 June 1995. Now let us suppose that on 20 June 1995, the UK exporter and the French purchaser agree that settlement will take place on 31 July 1995. What the British exporter needs to do now is to counter the original forward sale of francs for settlement on 30 June and replace it with a contract for delivery on 31 July. This he does by buying FFr5m forward for delivery on 30 June 1995 (thereby creating a contra to his original forward sale of francs) and simultaneously selling FFr5m forward 41 days, thereby extending delivery to 31 July. Let us further assume that on 20 June 1995, the bank gives the UK exporter the following quotes:

Spot	7.94–7.95
10 days forward	¼ c–½ c discount
1 month forward	½ c–¾ c discount
41 days forward	¾ c–1 c discount

Turning these quotes into full forward data, remembering that the bid/offer spread is wider in the forward market than in the spot market, we obtain:

Spot	7.94–7.95
10 days forward	7.9425–7.9550
1 month forward	7.9450–7.9575
41 days forward	7.9475–7.9600

Thus the overall covering mechanism can be seen to involve the following transactions:

1 May 1995	Sell FFr5m for £ forward 2 months at 7.87⅜ (delivery 30 June 1995)	£635,021
20 June 1955	Buy FFr5m for £ forward 10 days at 7.9425 (delivery 30 June 1995)	(629,525)
20 June 1995	Sell FFr5m for £ forward 41 days at 7.96 (delivery 31 July 1995)	628,141
	Net sterling proceeds	£633,637

As can be seen from the above, leg two of the total mechanism reverses leg one. Legs two and three are the opposite sides of the forward swap.

The effect of the above forward swap deal is that the British exporter has locked in as of 1 May 1995 at the forward rate for two months' cover adjusted for the premium/discount for a further month given by the bid/offer spread incurred on the forward/forward swap. Of course, as at 1 May 1995 the exporter does not know what the premium/discount will be on extending the contract, nor will he know what the bid/offer spread will be on the swap. The unknown premium/discount is a function of interest rate differentials prevailing on Eurosterling and Euro-French francs at the date when the forward swap is done.

This forward swap deal will mean that on the first two legs the UK exporter makes a profit which will be received from the bank on 30 June

1995. The UK exporter's cash flow on the foreign exchange cover becomes:

30 June 1995	Profit received from bank	£ 5,496
31 July 1995	Sale of receivable at 7.96	628,141
		£633,637

Rather than doing a forward/forward deal, the bank would be prepared to roll the contract for their customer. Rolling this old contract forward would work as follows. The market rate for rolling the contract forward by one month is 1.75 centimes (7.96 less 7.9425). So the bank will adjust the original forward deal by 1.75 centimes. For settlement on 31 July 1995, the bank would charge 7.89⅛ and the sterling proceeds, payable on 31 July 1995, would be:

$$\frac{5,000,000}{7.89125} = £633,613$$

This amount is approximately the same as from the forward/forward swap. Differences are frequently much greater than the small variation in our example. However, the rolling process illustrated above is approximate and it can cost the bank's customer dear at times. The swap mechanism is always cheaper for the customer.

A spot/forward swap is similar to a forward swap. It again involves a simultaneous pair of foreign exchange contracts, one of which is a spot contract while the other is a forward contract. Reverting to our numerical example, the original forward deal would be for the arbitrarily set two-month period. But the exporter would wait until 30 June 1995 to reverse this deal and to extend maturity to the expected settlement date, namely 31 July 1995. The mechanism might then be summarized as:

1 May 1995	Sell FFr5m for £ forward 2 months at 7.87⅜ (delivery 30 June)	£635,021
30 June 1995	Buy FFr5m for £ spot at (say) 8.05	(621,118)
30 June 1995	Sell FFr5m for £ forward 31 days at (say) 8.0725 (delivery 31 July 1995)	619,387
	Net sterling proceeds	£633,290

The above figuring assumes that the spot rate to buy French francs as of 30 June 1995 had moved to 8.0500 and the one-month forward rate as of that date had become 8.0725 to sell francs for sterling. Had the customer rolled the old contract forward on 30 June 1995, the proceeds as of 31 July would have been:

$$\frac{5,000,000}{7.89625} = £633,212$$

Again, this is not far out compared with the spot/forward method.

In practice, the forward/forward or spot/forward swap is the preferred method of dealing with uncertain settlement dates. But the option forward contract is a useful mechanism for dealing with a continuing stream of foreign currency payments or receipts. Where a firm's sales include a large number of small transactions denominated in foreign currency terms, it is expensive both in transaction and administrative costs to cover each individual deal. This problem may be overcome by taking out a single, large forward option contract to cover the approximate expected total cash value of the large number of different receivables or payables. Although the large number of small exports would normally have different settlement dates, forward options are ideally suited to this kind of situation. The amount of the forward contract is usually rounded off. Because of this, it is usually necessary to close out bulk forward contracts of this sort by a spot purchase or sale to balance amounts due from or to the bank.

As an example, assume that a British exporter is expecting a series of Austrian schilling receipts during the course of the six months from 10 January to 10 July. This rough total is estimated at AS10m. To cover this, the exporter sells AS10m on a six-month forward option with the option over the whole period. Assume that the rate is AS 15.61 to the pound and that the Austrian schilling receipts delivered from proceeds of sales are as follows:

16 Feb.	AS2.4m @ 15.61 =	£153,748
21 Mar.	AS2.6m @ 15.61 =	166,560
16 June	AS3.1m @ 15.61 =	198,591
21 June	AS1.5m @ 15.61 =	96,092

Sterling proceeds from AS9.6m @ 15.61 = £614,991

Thus the exporter has delivered AS9.6m. If no more schilling receipts come in from sales up to 10 July, the exporter must close out the deal by buying in AS400,000 in the spot market on that date and delivering this against the balance of the forward option contract. If the spot rate on 10 July is AS15.25, then the receipts for the forward option come out at:

Sterling proceeds from sale of AS9.6m (as above)	£614,991
Cost of buying in AS0.4m on 10 July at spot rate of AS15.25	(26,230)
Sterling proceeds from sale of AS0.4m at AS15.61	25,625
Net sterling proceeds	£614,386

Had our exporter actually received in excess of the AS10m during the forward option period, the excess would be sold spot for sterling.

Short-term borrowing

Short-term borrowing provides an alternative way of covering a receivable or payable denominated in a foreign currency. The availability of this technique as a practical tool of exposure management is subject to local credit availability and transactions must conform to exchange controls, which may restrict its use.

The mechanism is best illustrated by a numerical example and for this purpose we return to the date in Figure 8.1. Our UK exporter had a three-month exposure of FFr5m from the contract date of 1 May 1995, through to settlement date on 31 July 1995. Assume that the exporter decides to use short-term borrowing to cover the transaction exposure. Simultaneous with the signing of the contract, he should borrow a sum in French francs such that with interest the expected receipt of FFr5m in three months' time will repay the principal and accrued interest. This French franc sum should be switched immediately to sterling via the spot market. With French franc three-month interest rates equal to $5\frac{3}{32}$ per cent per annum, the sum to borrow would be FFr4,937,129, since this would mean that FFr5m would be payable to clear the loan and interest in three months' time. Converting the borrowing to sterling at the spot rate of FFr7.935 = £1 would yield £622,196 and if this were immediately put on deposit at the UK investment rate of 10 per cent per annum, this would grow to £637,751 (given by £622,196 × 1.025) at the end of three months. This is approximately the same as the yield on the forward transaction (see Figure 8.1).

In practice, it might be the case that our exporter decided to borrow FFr5m on the signing of the contract and at the same date to buy FFr63,672 forward (made up as FFr5m × $5\frac{3}{32}$ per cent per annum × $\frac{3}{12}$). He would simultaneously sell the FFr5m for sterling via the spot market. Thus the UK exporter is completely covered against exchange risk. On 31 July 1995 the UK company receives FFr5m from its French customer and this is used to repay principal of the French franc borrowing. The exporter simultaneously receives FFr63,672 from the forward contract and this amount is used to cover accrued interest. All these transactions can be tied in at rates determined on 1 May 1995. Then rates are unaffected by subsequent currency and/or interest rate movements over the exposure period. If the proceeds of the FFr5m borrowing are switched to sterling at the spot rate on 1 May 1995, the overall proceeds of the deal are as follows:

1 May 1995	Borrow FFr5m at $5\frac{3}{32}$ per cent p.a.	
	Buy FFr63,672 forward 3 months at $7.83\frac{1}{8}$	
	Sell FFr5m spot to give £630,120 at $7.93\frac{1}{2}$	
	Invest £630,120 for 3 months at 10 per cent p.a.	
31 July 1995	Receive FFr5m from customer; use this to repay principal of loan	
	Deliver FFr63,672 to cover loan interest	
	This comes from forward contract	(£8,131)
	Receive proceeds of sterling loan given by £630,120 at 10 per cent p.a. for 3 months	645,873
	Net sterling proceeds	£637,742

The slightly different proceeds from this transaction arise because the amount borrowed is FFr5m as opposed to FFr4.937m.

By this kind of mechanism, any receivable or payable which can be covered by a forward contract may be covered by short-term borrowing, assuming credit is available and that exchange controls do not prohibit any leg of the transaction.

Just as we looked at imprecise settlement dates and how to cover these via a forward option, so we can cover this eventuality by taking an overdraft type of loan. Rather than doing a forward option for, say, between three and six months, we could arrange an overdraft borrowing for the amount of a receivable for a period of up to six months and remit the proceeds of the borrowing via the spot market to the home country. A complication arises because interest rates on overdraft loans float up and down. Consequently, interest payable cannot be tied in for certain. Interest is usually catered for by a spot transaction, after the event, namely at the date when the borrowing is repaid. But by the same token, the proceeds of the borrowing remitted to the home country via the spot market will earn interest and this will vary according to market conditions in the home country. The interest payable and receivable may both be left to market conditions at floating rates.

Earlier in this chapter we considered briefly how a continuing stream of foreign currency exposures could be covered using the forward market. This kind of situation can also be covered via short-term borrowing. The company in the home country arranges a borrowing facility in the currency of invoicing. This technique can be used simultaneously to handle the problems of continuing foreign currency exposures and uncertain settlement dates. Assume that we have a UK exporter with a continuing stream of Austrian schilling export receipts. These can be covered by arranging a fixed rate schilling borrowing. When each export contract is finalized the exporter immediately draws down the schilling loan by the amount of the sale and converts the proceeds into sterling. As the receivables are settled, the schillings are paid into the exporter's schilling account so that the borrowing is reduced. As long as the schilling borrowing rate is fixed over the exposure term, the receivable is fully covered against exchange risk.

Discounting foreign currency denominated bills receivable

Discounting can be used to cover export receivables. Where an export receivable is to be settled by a bill of exchange, the exporter may discount the bill and thereby receive payment before the settlement date. The bill may be discounted either with a bank in the customer's country, in which case the foreign currency proceeds can be repatriated immediately at the current spot rate, or it can be discounted with a bank in the exporter's country so that the exporter may receive settlement direct in home currency. Either way, the exporter is covered against exchange risk, the cost being the discount rate charged by the bank.

Factoring foreign currency denominated receivables

Like discounting, factoring can be used for covering export receivables. When the export receivable is to be settled on open account, rather than by a bill of exchange, the receivable can be assigned as collateral for bank financing. Normally such a service gives protection against exchange rate changes, though during unsettled periods in the foreign exchange markets appropriate variations in the factoring agreement are usual. Commercial banks and specialized factoring institutions offer factoring services. For the exporter, the technique is very straightforward: he simply sells his export receivables to the factor and receives home currency in return. The costs involved include credit risks, the cost of financing, and the cost of covering exchange risk. For these reasons, factoring tends to be an expensive means of covering exposure, although there may be offsetting benefits such as obtaining export finance and reducing sales accounting and credit collection costs.

Currency overdrafts

Overdrafts in Eurocurrencies are available in the London money markets in all of the major currencies although banks tend to specialize by currency. The US dollar and the Deutsche Mark are the currencies in which the greatest amounts are advanced.

In terms of avoidance of exposure, all that a company needs to do is to maintain the amount of its foreign currency receivables in a particular currency equal to the balance on the overdraft in that currency. However, if the company uses the proceeds of the receivables to run down the overdraft, then it also needs to draw down the foreign currency loan as sales denominated in foreign currency are made. Some companies find it more convenient to sell the proceeds of foreign denominated receivables spot rather than to be perpetually adjusting the level of the overdraft. However, if the level of the currency overdraft remains constant, there is an assumption that new sales denominated in foreign currency are exactly offsetting incoming foreign receipts. This may not be realistic. If this is the case then, even with this method, it becomes necessary to refer to the level of foreign currency receivables and increase or run down the overdraft to ensure that exposure is being covered.

The currency overdraft is a particularly useful and economical technique of exposure management where a company carries a large number of small items denominated in foreign currency, all with uncertain payment dates.

In some countries, use of the currency overdraft exposure management technique may be limited by exchange controls which prevent residents from using foreign currency denominated bank accounts.

Another similar technique is the currency bank account. This is particularly useful where a company engaged in international trade has receivables in excess of payables in the same currency. The company opens a foreign currency denominated deposit account into which receivables in a particular currency are paid and out of which foreign denominated payments in that currency are made. For example, should a UK company have a US dollar receivable of $2m due on 31 October and should it also have a payment to be made on 30 November of $1.5m, the company might open a dollar denominated deposit account in which it pays the $2m. Of this, $½m would be remitted via a previously arranged forward deal for delivery on 31 October and $1½m would remain in the account to meet the payment due on 30 November. In addition, at the end of November some interest would have accrued on the US dollar bank account.

This kind of exercise is designed to save making a large number of forward deals which are priced to the bank's customer on the basis of the worst rate during a future period. In the above example, the trader received

US dollar interest on the deposit left in the currency account. Had he remitted all proceeds from the initial receivable to the UK, he could have obtained a UK interest rate on the proceeds. It can be seen that the essential net saving for the company arises from eliminating the bid/offer spread on amounts left in the currency account to meet future payables. However, a careful comparison should be made of the expected proceeds from the currency account technique with both the outturns from doing a large number of forward deals and the payoff from a forward option since the currency account may not always be the best choice. Remember that the pricing of forward deals is based on interbank Eurocurrency interest differentials, and using markets based on these differentials may give a superior result to the reliance on bank deposit accounts.

Government exchange risk guarantees

As part of a series of encouragements to exporters, government agencies in many countries offer their business insurance against export credit risks and certain export financing schemes. Many of these agencies offer exchange risk insurance to their exporters as well as the usual export credit guarantees. The exporter pays a small premium and in return the government agency absorbs all exchange risk, thereby taking profits and absorbing losses.

The precise details vary from one export finance agency to another and the exact offerings should be checked with such bodies as ECGD in the UK, HERMES in West Germany, COFACE in France, Netherlands Credit Insurance Company in Holland, Eximbank in the USA and so on. Nowadays, most countries have export credit and other similar government agencies offering to absorb foreign exchange exposure risk on export and import transactions in return for a fee.

An overview

External techniques of foreign exchange exposure management use contractual relationships outside of a group of companies in order to reduce the risk of losses from exchange rate changes.

The most well known of these involves the forward currency market, which may be used not only to cover receivables and payables but also to speculate on foreign currency movements. Although this market may be used to cover a receipt or payment denominated in a foreign currency when the date of receipt or payment is known, it can readily be adapted to allow for situations when the exact payment date is unknown. Techniques here include the forward option, the forward/forward swap, and the spot/forward swap. It should be noted that a forward option (or option forward as it is sometimes called) is not a currency option. A forward option involves a right and an obligation to deal in foreign currency; the option is merely as to timing. Currency swaps and currency options are the focus of following chapters.

Short-term borrowing is another technique for covering receivables and payables, and cover may also be bought by discounting foreign currency denominated bills of exchange, by factoring foreign currency denominated receivables and by purchasing government exchange risk guarantees.

9

What are currency swaps?

In the previous chapter we introduced forward/forward swaps and spot/forward swaps. It is a little confusing but these are altogether different from currency and interest rate swaps. Basically swaps involve the exchange of interest or foreign currency exposures or a combination of both by two or more borrowers. They do not necessarily involve the legal swapping of actual debts but an agreement is made to meet certain cash flows under loan or lease agreements. What, in practical terms, does this mean?

Swaps

To illustrate how currency swaps work, consider a borrower who is in a relatively favourable position to raise long-term fixed rate US dollar funding but, in fact, wants floating rate yen. Assume another borrower of relatively high standing in the yen market but who does not have similar access to long-term fixed rate dollars but is seeking US dollar finance. A gain may accrue to each corporation by raising finance in the market in which they are each well known and then swapping liabilities. Via this route, both companies obtain finance in the denomination that they want at a rate cheaper than they would have been able to access directly. They have each traded market imperfections. The effect is to broaden the access of borrowers to international lending markets. Swaps help the corporate treasurer to manage his portfolio of liabilities. Essentially, currency swaps enable the treasurer to alter the mix of his liabilities and assets.

Swap transactions may be set up with great speed and their documentation and formalities are generally much less detailed than in comparable loan deals. Swap agreements are normally shorter and simpler than those relating to term loan agreements. Transaction costs are relatively low too. They are unlikely to exceed ½ per cent of the total sum. Furthermore, swaps can be unwound easily.

In analysing the swap markets, it is possible to distinguish four distinct classes of swap:

1. The interest rate swap.
2. The fixed rate currency swap.
3. The currency coupon swap.
4. The basis rate swap.

The combined total of swaps represents $700bn of new business per year and it is growing fast. The interest rate swap is the largest segment of the market worth over $600bn per annum. Set out below are the essential features of each of the above kinds of swap.

Interest rate swaps

Interest rate swaps involve the exchange between two counterparties of fixed rate interest for floating rate interest in the same currency calculated by reference to an agreed notional amount of principal. This principal amount applies only for the purpose of calculating the interest to be exchanged under an interest rate swap. At no time is any principal amount physically passed between the parties. The exchange of fixed for floating rate interest payment is made by reference to prevailing fixed and floating rates available in the marketplace, due account being taken of credit standing. The counterparties are thus able to convert a fixed rate asset or liability into a floating rate asset or liability and vice versa. Cost savings are obtained by each party.

The essential mechanism of interest rate swaps is fairly easy to understand. Usually, investors in fixed rate instruments are more sensitive to credit quality than are floating rate lenders. Thus a larger premium is demanded of issuers of lower credit quality in the fixed rate debt market than in the floating rate market. The counterparties to an interest rate swap effectively obtain an arbitrage advantage by drawing down funds in the market where they have the greater relative cost advantage, subsequently entering into an interest rate swap to convert the cost of the funds so raised from a fixed rate to a floating rate and vice versa.

The methodology of the arbitrage and its cost-saving potential can be seen by reference to an example involving two companies, X and Y. The former has a higher credit rating, as can be seen by the data in Figure 9.1. Its superior credit standing gives it a 110 basis point advantage in the fixed

	Company X	Company Y
Credit rating	AAA	BBB
Cost of direct fixed rate funding	10.40%	11.50%
Cost of direct floating rate funding	Six month LIBOR +0.25%	Six month LIBOR +0.75%
Funds raised directly		
Fixed rate by company X	(10.40%)	
Floating rate by company Y		(Six month LIBOR) +0.75%
Swap payments		
Company X pays company Y	(Six month LIBOR)	Six month LIBOR
Company Y pays company X	10.45%	(10.45%)
All-in cost of funding	Six month LIBOR −0.05%	11.20%
Comparable cost of direct funding	Six month LIBOR +0.25%	11.50%
Saving	30 basis points	30 basis points

Figure 9.1 Interest rate swap example.

rate funding market and a 50 basis point advantage in the floating rate market. In money market jargon, 100 basis points equals 1 per cent. Despite the fact that company X can raise funds more cheaply than company Y in both markets, a potential for an interest rate arbitrage exists. Company X draws down funds in the fixed rate market while company Y borrows on a floating basis. Each then enters into an interest rate swap requiring the payments from one to the other as shown under the heading of swap payments in Figure 9.1. It can be seen, by comparing the all-in cost of funding line in the exhibit with the details shown on the line headed 'comparable cost of direct funding', that each party has saved 30 basis points on the swap. The interest rate flows are summarized in Figure 9.2 in which the direction of the arrows represents the direction of interest rate flows.

The ability to transfer relative cost advantages in the manner shown in Figures 9.1 and 9.2 has led to many highly creditworthy companies issuing fixed rate Eurobonds solely with the purpose of swapping and frequently obtaining funding at an effective sub-LIBOR cost.[1] In the early phase of the interest rate swap market, a triple A issuer could expect to achieve between 75 and 100 basis points below LIBOR – the rate at which banks offer money to each other – on a swap. Nowadays, gains for a comparable borrower might bring the cost of funding down to 15 basis points below LIBOR.

Besides providing cost advantages, interest rate swaps enable borrowers

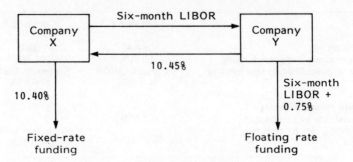

Figure 9.2 Direction of interest flows.

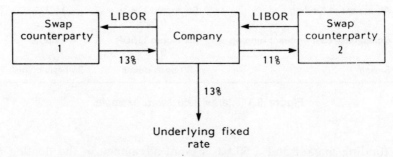

Figure 9.3 Position of company following two swaps.

effectively to access markets which might otherwise be closed to them, for example by virtue of credit quality or lack of a familiar name in a particular market segment. Also, private companies are enabled to tap particular markets without the need to comply with disclosure requirements, credit ratings and other formal requirements. Swaps based upon commercial paper as the underlying floating rate instrument are also a segment of the interest rate swap market.

Interest rate swaps may be used as a means of reducing interest rate exposure or as a pure financing tool. They may also be used to enable corporate treasurers to back their judgement on future trends in interest rates. For example, consider a company with fixed rate debt costing 13 per cent per annum at a time when the treasurer expects a decline in interest rates to occur. The company might enter into a swap to obtain LIBOR-based funding and leave this swap in place during the period when interest rates were falling. At the end of the decline, the company might enter into a second swap to lock into the new lower fixed rate of, say, 11 per cent per annum. The company's position would then be like that summarized in Figure 9.3.

The interest rate swap process has the advantage of utter simplicity. It is often conducted by telephone, confirmed by telex subject to agreement on documentation which usually incorporates the minimum of restrictive covenants. There are both primary and secondary interest rate swap markets. The market centres on New York, London and Tokyo.

Currency swaps

We now turn to the fixed rate currency swap, which is the oldest of the four subclassifications of swap market. A fixed rate currency swap involves one counterparty exchanging fixed rate interest in one currency with another counterparty in return for fixed rate interest in another currency. Currency swaps usually involve three basic steps:

1. Initial exchange of principal.
2. Ongoing exchange of interest.
3. Re-exchange of principal amounts on maturity.

The initial exchange of principal works as follows. At the outset, the counterparties exchange the principal amounts of the swap at an agreed rate of exchange. This rate is usually based on the spot exchange rate. This initial exchange can be on a notional basis, that is with no physical exchange of principal amounts. The counterparties simply convert principal amounts into the required currency via the spot market. Whether the initial exchange is on a physical or notional basis, its importance is solely to establish the reference point of the principal amounts for the purpose of calculating first the ongoing payments of interest and second the re-exchange of principal amounts, at maturity, under the swap.

The ongoing exchange of interest is the second key step in the currency swap. Having established the principal amounts, the counterparties exchange interest payments on agreed dates based on the outstanding principal amounts at the fixed interest rates agreed at the outset of the transaction.

The third step in the currency swap involves the re-exchange of principal amounts. Agreement on this enables the counterparties to re-exchange the principal sums at the maturity date.

This three-step process is standard practice in the currency swap market and it in effect transforms a fixed rate debt raised in one currency into a fixed rate liability in another currency.

The swap of fixed interest in one currency for fixed interest in another simply draws on market rates for the maturity concerned in the particular currencies. The interest rate difference is based upon Fisher effect considerations as set out earlier in this book (see Chapter 2).

The most important currencies in the currency swap market are the US dollar, the Swiss franc, the Deutsche Mark, the ECU, sterling and the Canadian dollar. The market is dominated by the US dollar on one side but direct swaps have been frequent in yen/Swiss franc, yen/ECU, Deutsche Mark/Swiss franc and there are many others too. The currency swap is one further tool which enables corporate treasurers to manage currency exposures and reap cost benefits at the same time.

Currency coupon swaps

The third class of swap, the currency coupon swap, is essentially a combination of the interest rate swap and the fixed rate currency swap. The transaction follows the three basic steps described for the fixed rate currency swap with the exception that fixed rate interest in one currency is exchanged for floating rate interest in another currency – again based upon prevailing market rate considerations and credit rating.

Basis rate swaps

The final classification of swap is the basis rate swap. The structure of the basis rate swap is the same as the straight interest rate swap except that floating interest calculated on one basis is exchanged for floating interest calculated on a different basis. The origin of this kind of swap was the US dollar prime rate/LIBOR swap. However, a larger market has developed for the exchange of one month US dollar LIBOR for six months US dollar LIBOR and also the exchange of US dollar LIBOR for US dollar commercial paper.

An overview

Swaps simply involve the exchange of currency or interest rate exposures by reference to prevailing money and foreign exchange market rates. Interest rate swaps involve exchanging a fixed rate exposure for floating rate payments (or vice versa) in the same currency. Prevailing market rates underpin the swap. Fixed rate currency swaps involve exchanging a fixed rate interest exposure in one currency for a fixed rate exposure in another – rates in each currency draw upon market rates as does the initial exchange of currency. Likewise, currency coupon swaps and basic rate swaps draw on market rates to underpin the swap.

The swap market enables corporate treasurers to pursue a number of profitable tactics. These embrace:

1. Accessing prevailing money market rates which would not otherwise be available except at prohibitive rates.
2. Converting exposures in one currency into another; as such it enables the treasurer to achieve many of the features that the forward market makes available.
3. Insuring against interest rate and currency rate changes by converting exposures of one kind to another.
4. Speculating on interest rate and currency rate changes.
5. Accessing money market imperfections, thereby raising finance at rates below market rates otherwise available.

Note

1. LIBOR (London Interbank Offer Rate) is the interest rate at which prime banks offer deposits to other prime banks in London.

10

What are financial futures on foreign exchange?

A financial futures contract is an agreement to buy or sell a standard quantity of a specific financial instrument at a future date and at a price agreed between the parties through open outcry on the floor of an organized financial futures exchange. With respect to standard quantity, each contract for a given type of financial instrument is for the same standard quantity, for example $100,000. The term 'specific financial instrument' implies that the contract specification lays down the type of financial instrument (for example a twenty-year gilt-edged stock with a stated interest rate, or a foreign currency) with delivery at an explicit maturity. With respect to future date, the delivery of the amounts specified in the contract must take place on one of four specified dates in the forthcoming year. The vast majority of financial futures deals are reversed before delivery date: thus most purchase deals are reversed by matching sale deals, thereby avoiding the need for delivery physically to be effected. Standardization as to quantity and type of instrument enables easy transferability of futures contracts. Financial futures contracts can be sold via the financial futures exchange.

Financial futures in general

Someone who buys an interest rate future has the right and obligation to deposit money to the nominal amount contracted for at a specified interest rate for a specified period with the seller. Someone who sells an interest rate future makes himself available to take a deposit amounting to the nominal amount contracted at a specified rate of interest for a specific period of time.

Trading in financial futures markets is by open outcry as opposed to by telephone or telex, which is the usual means in the forward markets. A principal may give instructions to his broker by telephone but the broker will effect the deal for his client on the financial futures floor (or pit, as it is called). Users transact business only through authorized brokers, who receive a commission.

A clearing house exists to ease the funds flow from the execution of contracts. In financial futures trading, the clearing house evolved to assume the credit risk in futures transactions by guaranteeing the performance of buyer and seller to each other.

While all financial futures transactions must have a buyer and seller, their obligation is not to each other but to a clearing house. After a transaction is recorded, the clearing house substitutes itself for the other party and becomes the seller to every buyer and the buyer to every seller. In this way the clearing house achieves its primary objective, which is to guarantee the performance of every transaction done on the floor of the financial futures exchange. Trading on margin is a feature of financial futures. Only a small fraction, called the initial margin, of the underlying instrument's value has to be put up initially by the purchaser or seller as security for performance. This amount varies according to the contract which is being dealt in, but it is typically between 1 and 5 per cent of the instrument's value. Clearly, this produces gearing which may be attractive to market operators. Gearing acts to the advantage of the operator in terms of magnifying his gains when markets are moving in his favour. But the reverse holds when markets move against the operator. Margin positions are revised daily, accounts are debited or credited according to movements and margin calls are made to cover accrued losses and to top up subsequent margin to the required percentage level. The essential differences between the mechanics of financial futures and forward foreign exchange transactions are summarized in Table 10.1.

Financial futures provide a means of hedging for those who wish to lock in currency exchange rates on future currency transactions. So foreign currency receivables and payables may be hedged via financial futures if a market exists in the foreign and home currency. In fact, financial futures markets in foreign currencies exist for only a small spectrum of currencies; these are listed later in this chapter.

Financial futures may be traded by those who are willing to assume risk and wish to profit from the rises or falls they expect to occur in interest rates or exchange rates. This enables users to take a view about trends in rates without actually having to purchase or sell the underlying currency or financial instrument. They may sell a contract which they do not already own (going short) when they feel that it is likely that interest rates will rise or a currency's value will decline. The operator hopes to buy the contract in after a fall in its price prior to the delivery date, thereby making a profit.

Hedgers and speculators each have an important role to play in creating efficient operations in financial futures markets. Traders (or speculators)

Table 10.1 Comparison of forward and futures markets in foreign exchange

	Financial futures	Forward markets
Location	Future exchanges	Banks and other traders – no single location
Trading medium	Open outcry	Telephone/telex
Contract size	Standardized	As required by customer
Maturity/delivery date	Standardized	As required by customer
Counterparty	Clearing house	Known bank or other trader
Credit risk	Clearing house	Individual counterparty
Commissions	Always payable – flat rate for small deals; otherwise negotiable	Negotiable or implied in dealer's spread when no specific commission is payable
Security	Margin required	Counterparty credit risk; banks set this against credit limits according to their own house rules
Liquidity	Provided by margin payments	Provided by credit limits
Leverage	Very high	No formal gearing, but since payment is not required until delivery, although credit limits are used, gearing may in effect be achieved
Settlement	Via clearing house	Via arrangements with banks

provide liquidity to the market enabling hedgers to buy or sell in volume without difficulty. Only a small percentage of futures contracts is held until delivery. The reason for this is that most hedgers have no further need for the hedge once they have traded out of their position in the cash market. Traders usually close their position once they have achieved their profit objectives or decided to cut their losses. A buyer closes his position by making an offsetting sale of the same contract; a seller makes an offsetting purchase.

There are two key elements of cost involved in dealing in financial futures. These are direct costs and margin costs. Members charge a negotiated commission for executing orders for a customer. Commission is charged for a round trip. This covers both the opening and the closing of a position and is normally payable either when the position is closed or when delivery takes place. This is the direct cost element.

Margin works differently. When a deal has been done, both buyer and seller have to put up margin to the clearing house (either cash or collateral) to provide against adverse price movements of the futures contract. The minimum level of this margin, the initial margin, is set by the clearing house and reflects the volatility of the underlying instrument. Typically, margin may range from 1 to 5 per cent of the face value of the contract. As prices fluctuate daily, the value of outstanding contracts (open positions) will change. The amount of each day's gain or loss (called variation margin) is added to or subtracted from the margin account. Daily profits may be drawn by the investor. However, in order to maintain the initial margin intact, any losses have to be paid to the broker. Because the initial margin is greater than the likely daily movement of the underlying cash instruments, losses on a given day will not generally exceed the amount in a customer's margin account. If a contract is held until delivery, the buyer has to pay the seller the full value of the contract.

Currency contracts

We are concerned here with currency contracts traded on financial futures exchanges. For purposes of illustration we assume contracts for the dollar against sterling, the Deutsche Mark, the Swiss franc and the Japanese yen. Sizes and key data for such currency future contracts appear in Table 10.2.

Financial futures contracts in currencies are priced in terms of the underlying exchange rate. The sterling futures contract (that is, sterling against the US dollar) might be quoted one day at 1.6800 and at 1.6950 on the next day. The pricing system is similar to that in the foreign exchange market. Other LIFFE currency contracts in yen, Deutsche Marks and Swiss francs were quoted in terms of the number of dollars per unit of foreign currency, that is, equivalent to the direct quote as in New York. As shown in Table 10.2, the tick value if 0.01 cents per unit of foreign currency. The term tick refers to the minimum price movement in a contract – it is the last decimal place quoted by dealers. With this background, let us consider a simple example. A trader buys three sterling currency contracts at a price of $1.6800; he may find that within a week

Table 10.2 Currency futures contracts*

	Currency against US dollar			
	Sterling	Deutsche Mark	Swiss franc	Japanese yen
Unit of trading	£25,000	DM125,000-	SFr125,000	¥12,500,000
Delivery months	For all contracts, delivery months are March, June, September and December			
Delivery date	For all contracts, delivery is on the third Wednesday of delivery month			
Quotation	US$ per £	US$ per DM	US$ per SFr	US$ per ¥100
Minimum price movement	0.01 cents per £	0.01 cents per DM	0.01 cents per SFr	0.01 cents per ¥100
Tick size and value	$2.50	$12.50	$12.50	$12.50
Initial margin	$1,000	$1,000	$1,000	$1,000

*The contract sizes are the old LIFFE contracts which were suspended in 1990.

the position is closable at a price of $1.7300. This would yield a profit of $3,750, as calculated below:

3 contracts × 500 ticks

Or, put another way, profit equals:

$$\$\frac{(1.7300 - 1.6800)}{0.0001} \times 2.50 \text{ (\$ per tick)} \times 3 \text{ contracts}$$

= $3,750 (total profit)

The trader calculates his overall profit or loss by multiplying the number of contracts by the number of ticks of price change by the tick value. These three contracts would require initial margin of $3,000 and this would be outstanding for one week.

It should be noted that rates of initial margin quoted in Table 10.2 would apply only between clearing members of financial futures exchange and the clearing house. Margin arrangements for others may vary. A member may insist on being paid higher initial margins than those stated; the effect of this is to provide a cushion to cover variation margin calls and obviate the need for frequent charges or payments for small price changes on futures contracts. The key factor regarding margin is to know exactly how much cash will be needed to take up the desired futures position, and to relate interest forgone on financing the deal to potential trading profits.

The financial futures markets do not claim to be superior to forward markets in terms of covering foreign exchange risk. However, they may be used to enable a company respectively to cover a receivable or payable by selling or buying the appropriate foreign currency. Clearly there are disadvantages compared with forward markets. Financial futures markets have only four delivery dates per year; deals are done for standard quantities of currency; and only a small number of currencies are dealt. The problem of specific delivery dates can be overcome by trading a number of contracts for the next delivery date immediately beyond the exposure, and selling on such contracts when the receivable or payable is met.

Arbitraging between financial futures currency quotations and forward markets tends to lead to equality of quotations. So it should be the case that the profit or loss on the financial futures currency contract used to cover an exposure should approximate the profit or loss accruing where cover is achieved through the forward markets. Normally the proceeds from covering via forwards and futures are similar, but forward contracts use up credit lines negotiated with a bank whereas futures contracts do not.

Standardization of size of financial futures contracts is a problem for the corporate treasurer seeking cover for foreign exchange exposure via financial futures. This is easily overcome by taking that number of contracts which approximates the value of the desired exposed amount – but of course this method cannot yield an exact hedge.

The Chicago International Monetary Market (IMM) deals the following currencies against the US dollar: Mexican peso, Swiss franc, sterling, Deutsche Mark, Canadian dollar, Japanese yen, Dutch guilder, French franc and more too. UK-based brokers will readily arrange IMM contracts for clients wishing to do business in these markets. The range of contracts offered is expanding all the time as new financial futures centres open. For example, the Sydney Futures Exchange deals in the Australian dollar and the New Zealand Futures Exchange quotes a New Zealand dollar contract.

The financial futures markets are frequently used for currency trading and speculation. Trading may involve taking an uncovered position in a financial futures contract. This occurs when the trader backs his opinion that exchange rates are going to move in a particular direction and when he believes that the general expectations of rates which are reflected in the current level of futures prices do not fully, or even correctly, discount likely events enabling a position to be taken that will show a profit should rates move in the way the trader predicts.

An overview

Financial futures markets are used for trading and hedging. Trading refers to speculation on future price movements. Financial futures hedging is used to reduce the risk of loss through adverse price movements in interest rates, currency rates or share prices by taking a position that is equal and opposite to an existing exposure. Hedging allows parties to lock in to existing interest rates, currency rates or share prices even though an exposure is not incurred until some time in the future.

11

How do currency options work?

Currency options provide the right, but not the obligation, to buy or sell a specific currency at a specific price at any time prior to a specified date. That options provide 'the right but not the obligation' means that commercial users of the market are able to obtain insurance against an adverse movement in the exchange rate while still retaining the opportunity to benefit from favourable exchange movements. At the same time, the maximum risk to the buyer of an option is the actual up-front premium cost of the option. Currency options have not been designed as a substitute for forward markets but as a new, distinct financial vehicle that offers significant opportunities and advantages to those seeking either protection or profit from changes in exchange rates.

Since December 1982, the Philadelphia Stock Exchange has been trading standardized foreign currency option contracts. Philadelphia offers a competitive marketplace in which to buy and sell options against the US dollar on sterling, Deutsche Marks, Canadian dollars, Swiss francs, Japanese yen and French francs. Philadelphia was the first trading-centre to deal in currency options and it remains the world market leader although it has been joined by other centres such as the Chicago International Monetary Market, the Montreal Stock Exchange, the Amsterdam Stock Exchange and the London International Financial Futures Exchange (LIFFE). The International Monetary Market in Chicago trades currency options in the dollar against sterling, Deutsche Marks, and Swiss francs; Montreal offers US dollar currency options against sterling, the Deutsche Mark, Swiss francs, Japanese yen and Canadian dollars; Amsterdam deals in currency options for the dollar against sterling, Deutsche Marks, and Swiss francs; Montreal offers US dollar currency options against sterling, Deutsche Marks, Dutch guilders and the ECU; and LIFFE deals US dollar currency options against sterling and the Deutsche Mark. There are other centres too.

In this chapter we focus upon Philadelphia options. It begins with a description of how currency option markets work. This is linked with a discussion of currency option terminology and is followed by a discussion relating to currency option pricing. There is then a section devoted to use of currency options as risk-reducing instruments available to the corporate treasurer.

How currency option markets work

Philadelphia currency options are similar to options on ordinary shares. The buyer of an option cannot lose more than the cost of the option and is not subject to any margin calls. The Philadelphia Stock Exchange offers investors an organized marketplace in which to buy and sell options on sterling, Deutsche Marks, Canadian dollars, Swiss francs, Japanese yen, French francs, Australian dollars and ECUs, all against the US dollar. Options are traded on three-, six- and nine-month cycles – see Figure 11.1.

Currency option markets have a jargon of their own, although this language has much in common with that of traded options on shares. Because we shall frequently use the jargon in this chapter, a short list of currency options terms and definitions follows:

American option	An option which can be exercised on any business day within the option period.
European option	An option which can only be exercised on the expiry date.
A call option	An option to purchase a stated number of units of the underlying foreign currency at a specific price per unit during a specific period of time. By 'underlying foreign currency' we refer to the currency which is not the US dollar. Thus the term 'underlying foreign currency' could refer to sterling in the context of a US dollar/sterling currency option.
A put option	An option to sell a stated number of units of the underlying foreign currency at a specific price per unit during a specific period of time.
Option buyer	The party who obtains the benefit under an option by paying a premium. These benefits are the right, but not the obligation, to buy the currency if the option is a call or to sell the currency if the option is a put. The option buyer is known as the option holder.
Option seller	The party who has the obligation to perform if the option is exercised. This person will have to sell the foreign currency at a stated price if a call is exercised or buy the foreign currency at a stated price if a put is exercised. The original option seller is known as the option writer.

	Contract size
Philadelphia Stock Exchange *(Settlement dates: March, June, September, December)*	
Pounds sterling	£31,250
Deutsche Mark	DM62,500
Swiss franc	SFr62,500
Japanese yen	¥6,250,000
Canadian dollar	C$50,000
French franc	FFr250,000
Australian dollar	A$50,000
ECU	ECU62,500
Chicago Mercantile Exchange *(Settlement dates: March, June, September, December)*	
Deutsche Mark	DM125,000
Pounds sterling	£25,000
Swiss franc	Sfr125,000
Canadian dollar	C$100,000
Japanese yen	¥12,500,000
Options on currency futures	

Figure 11.1 Some of the currency options on the Philadelphia and Chicago exchanges.

Exercise price, exercise rate or strike price	The price at which the option holder has the right to purchase or sell the underlying currency. Except for the French franc and Japanese yen, exercise prices are stated in US cents. Thus a DM75 call would be an option to buy Deutsche Marks at $0.75 per Mark, that is DM1.33 = $1. Strike prices for options on the French franc are stated in tenths of a US cent. The holder of a FFr170 call option has a right to purchase the underlying French francs at $0.170 per franc. The Japanese yen option exercise prices are stated in hundredths of a cent, so a ¥67 call entitles the holder to purchase the underlying yen at $0.0067 per yen.
Expiration months	The expiration months for options are usually March, June, September and December. At any given time trading is available in the nearest three of these months.
Option premium	The option premium is the price of an option, that is the sum of money that the buyer of an option pays when an option is purchased or the

	sum that the writer of an option receives when an option is written.
Intrinsic value	The extent to which an option would currently be profitable to exercise. In the case of a call, if the spot price of the underlying currency is above the option exercise price, this difference is its intrinsic value. In the case of a put, if the spot price is below the option exercise price, this is its intrinsic value. Options with intrinsic value are said to be in-the-money. If the spot Deutsche Mark price is $0.75, a DM72 call would have an intrinsic value of $0.03 DM, but a DM72 put would have no intrinsic value.
Time value	That part of the premium representing the length of time that the option has to run. In other words, the premium less the intrinsic value.
Notice of exercise	Notice given by an option holder to an option writer that an option is being exercised. Only an option holder may exercise an option. The option holder may exercise his option and the option writer may be assigned a notice of exercise at any time prior to expiration of the option.
Opening transaction	A purchase or sale transaction which establishes an option's position.
Closing transaction	A transaction which liquidates or offsets an existing option's position. Option holders may liquidate their positions by an offsetting sale. An option writer may liquidate his position by an offsetting purchase.
At-the-money	An option whose exercise price is the same as the spot price.
Out-of-the-money	A call whose exercise price is above the current spot price of the underlying currency or a put option whose exercise price is below the current spot price of the underlying currency. Out-of-the-money options have no intrinsic value.
In-the-money	A call whose exercise price is below the current spot price of the underlying currency or a put whose exercise price is above the current spot price of the underlying currency. In-the-money options have intrinsic value.

Currency option contracts are standardized. Contract sizes on Philadelphia are set out in Figure 11.1 for each currency against the US dollar. When trading is introduced in an option with a new expiration month, the practice is for one option to be introduced with an exercise price above the current spot price and one to be introduced with an exercise price below the current spot price. As the spot price of a currency changes over time, additional options are introduced with the same expiration month but higher or lower exercise prices. The exercise price intervals are $0.01 for Deutsche Marks, Swiss francs and Canadian dollars, $0.05 for sterling and $0.0001 for Japanese yen and $0.005 for French francs.

Thus, if Deutsche Mark options with a September expiration are introduced when the spot price is $0.75, exercise prices would normally be established at 74, 75 and 76. If the spot price were to change to $0.76, a new series of options, having the same expiration date, would be introduced with an exercise price of 77.

Prices, or premia, for foreign exchange options are arrived at through competition between buyers and sellers on the floor of the Philadelphia Stock Exchange. The premium quoted represents a consensus opinion of the option's current value and will comprise either or both intrinsic value and time value. Option premium quotations have bid and offer rates like most financial exchange contracts.

Intrinsic value is the amount, if any, by which an option is currently in the money. Time value is that sum of money which buyers are willing to pay over and above any intrinsic value. Such buyers hope that, before expiration, the option will increase in value and may be sold or exchanged at a profit. If an option has no intrinsic value, its premium will be entirely a reflection of its time value.

The price or premium of an option reflects changes in the spot price of the underlying currency and the length of time remaining until expiration. Thus, with the spot Deutsche Mark price at $0.75, a DM73 call with three months until expiration may command a premium of $1,600. Of this, $1,250, given by $0.02 × DM62,500, is intrinsic value and the remaining $350 is time value. It can be seen from Figure 11.1 that the size of one Deutsche Mark contract is DM62,500. It should be borne in mind that an option is a wasting asset. Its sole value (if any) at expiration will be its intrinsic value. Without intrinsic value, it will expire worthless. Thus, if the Deutsche Mark spot price in the previous example is still $0.75 when the Deutsche Mark call expires, the value of the option will be its intrinsic value of $1,250; it can no longer have time value. Of course, if the spot price had fallen by expiration to $0.73 or below, the DM73 call option would expire as worthless. Reference to key readings on factors influencing option premia and their behaviour are briefly considered in the section headed 'Option pricing models'.

It should be noted that option premia are quoted in US cents per unit of the underlying currency with the exception of the Japanese yen and French franc. Thus an option premium quotation of 1.00 for a Deutsche Mark option is 1 cent per Mark. Each option is for a standardized value of DM62,500, so the total option premium would be $625 given by 62,500 × $0.01. An option premium quotation for the Deutsche Mark contract of 0.76 would represent $0.0076 per Deutsche Mark. The option premium would be $475 given by 62,500 × $0.0076.

Similarly, if the premium quoted for an option on sterling is 8.4, the total premium amount would be $2,625 given by 31,250 × $0.084 (£31,250 is the contract size of one Philadelphia sterling option). For a Japanese yen contract a premium quotation of 2.0 would be two-hundredths of a cent ($0.0002). The premium would thus be $1,250 given by 6,250,000 × $0.0002. It seems a little complicated at first, but the simple arithmetic for translating these quotations into the cost per option contract becomes second nature to investors trading in options.

Currency option markets aim to provide a continuously active and liquid market in put and call options on foreign currencies. Orders to buy and sell options on foreign currencies are transmitted through brokers to the trading floor of the exchange in the same way as transactions involving shares, but currency options, like other types of option, are investments not backed with a certificate of any sort.

Currency option strategies

This section outlines some strategies for buying and writing options on foreign currencies. First we consider a situation in which there is a profit potential in buying call options to exploit a foreign currency's strength or the dollar's weakness. A call option entitles the holder to purchase units of the foreign currency at the option price stated in US dollars. The option holder will therefore make a profit if the value of the option at expiration is greater than the premium paid to acquire the option. Put another way, profit will accrue if the spot market price of the currency is above the option exercise price plus the initial option premium. As an example, assume that in March an investor pays $750 to buy a DM September 75 call and by the expiration date in September, the Deutsche Mark spot price has risen to 78, that is $0.78. The call option with an exercise price of 75, that is $0.75, gives the investor the right to purchase Deutsche Marks at 3 cents below their current market value; thus the option is in-the-money by 3 cents. Consequently, through selling or exercising the option, the investor will realize $1,875 given by $0.03 × 62,500. This amount less the $750 originally paid for the option produces a profit of $1,125 over a six-month period. If the Deutsche Mark spot price at expiration had been $0.75 or below, the option would have expired worthless. The investor would have lost all of the $750 premium; but under no circumstance could his loss have exceeded the $750 paid for the option.

If the initial premium cost of a DM75 call in $750, the following tabulation indicates the investor's profit or loss depending upon the Deutsche Mark spot price at the time the option expires.

DM spot rate at expiration	Profit or (loss) in US dollars
$0.75 or below	($750)
0.76	(125)
0.77	500
0.78	1,125
0.79	1,750
0.80	2,375
0.81	3,000
0.82	3,625
0.83	4,250

The presence of high gearing for relatively low risk is evident from the above figures. The call option buyer has an unlimited profit potential, whereas his potential loss is fixed at the cost of the option itself.

Of course, even when purchase of a call option is indicated, the investor seeking to profit from the currency change must still decide which call option to invest in. Options differ in the length of time remaining until expiration and in their exercise price. On a given date in April, there will be trading in Deutsche Mark options expiring in June, September and December. Assuming a Deutsche Mark spot price of $0.75, options may be available with exercise prices ranging from $0.75 to $0.77.

Options with more distant expiration months command a higher premium because they provide more time for the investor's expectations to be realized – that is, greater time value. Thus, an at-the-money DM75 call with three months to expiration may command a premium of $750. A DM75 option with six months to expiration may be priced at $1,150 and a similar option with nine months to expiration may cost $1,500.

In-the-money options always cost more than at-the-money options which in turn cost more than out-of-the-money options. Although the in-the-money option costs most in terms of investment, it also yields the greatest profit potential for any given increase of a foreign currency against the dollar.

There is no formula for arriving at an answer to the question of which option to select. The key thing to bear in mind is that for a call option buyer to make a net profit at expiration, the spot currency price must be above the option exercise price by an amount greater than the premium paid for the option.

Just as call options provide profit opportunities, so put options can do the same. Thus, investors expecting a particular currency to decline in value relative to the US dollar may seek to profit by the purchase of put options. These options convey the right, but not the obligation, to sell the foreign currency at an agreed price. Assume that at a time when the Deutsche Mark spot price is $0.75, an investor expecting the Deutsche Mark to weaken relative to the US dollar pays $450 to purchase an at-the-money DM75 put option with six months to run. Should the Deutsche Mark have dropped by expiration to, say, $0.72, the option may be sold or exercised at its intrinsic value of $1,875 and the investor's profit will be $1,425.

Assuming the investor pays a premium of $450 to purchase a Deutsche Mark put option with an exercise price of 75, the table below indicates his profit potential at various expiration spot prices:

DM spot rate at expiration	Profit or (loss) in US dollars
$0.75 or above	($450)
0.74	175
0.73	800
0.72	1,425
0.71	2,050
0.70	2,675
0.69	3,300
0.68	3,925
0.67	4,550

Considerations involved in buying put options are the inverse of those applicable to call options. Again, an option with a long period of time until expiry normally commands a higher premium than an otherwise identical option soon to expire. It is worth bearing in mind that the premium for an out-of-the-money option is low because such an option is less likely to become profitable to exercise.

Like traded options on shares, it is possible to write currency options for investment income. The writer of an option is obligated, if the option is exercised, to perform according to the terms of the option contract. Thus, the writer must sell and deliver the required number of units of the underlying currency at the option exercise price, if the option is a call, or purchase the required number of units at the option exercise price if the option is a put. Investors considering writing options must remember that holders of an option may exercise their rights under the option at any time (for an American option). Of course, option writing (unless covered) involves substantial and potentially unlimited risk. The limited risk of option trading applies only to the option buyer, not to the option writer. However, the terms of an option can make option writing a potentially attractive source of profit.

There are ways in which writers of currency options can cover themselves. The detail of covering strategies is outside the scope of this book. Interested readers may obtain an insight into the underlying

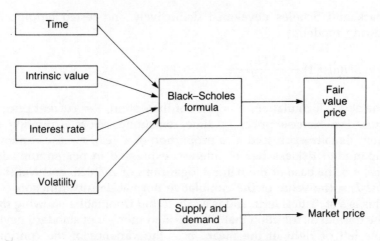

Figure 11.2 How an option is priced.

methodology by reference to *Multinational Finance* by Adrian Buckley (Prentice Hall, 1996).

Option pricing models

A mathematical model for pricing stock market traded options has been developed by Fischer Black and Myron Scholes (see 'The pricing of options and corporate liabilities', *Journal of Political Economy*, May/June 1973). The Black and Scholes model has been adapted to price currency options by Garman and Kohlhagen (see their paper 'Foreign currency option values', *Journal of International Money and Finance*, 1983). Both articles are hard work for the non-mathematician. Option pricing is logical and readily done with rigorous maths and follows the routine summarized in Figure 11.2. It is perhaps worth spending a little time explaining the option pricing model developed by Black and Scholes. The assumptions in deriving their model are important. These are as follows:

1. The option can be exercised at maturity only.
2. There are no transaction costs and no taxes.
3. The risk-free rate of interest is constant for the life of the option.
4. The shares in the company to which the option relates carry no cash dividends.
5. Share prices follow a random walk and the variance of the return on the share is constant over the life of the option. The variance can, for the purpose of the model, be estimated using past data.

Black and Scholes developed deductively and tested empirically the following model:

$$C = SN(dist\ 1) - \frac{EN(dist\ 2)}{e^{rt}}$$

In the above formulation, C = price of the option, S = current price of the shares, E = exercise price, t = time remaining before expiration of the option, usually expressed as a proportion of a year, r = the continuously compounded riskless rate of interest, expressed in per annum, decimal terms, e = the base of the natural logarithm, or 2.71828, and $N(dist\ 1)$ and $N(dist\ 2)$ = the value of the cumulative normal density function.

This is a statistical term and is easily found from tables showing the area of the normal distribution that is a specified number of standard deviations to the left or right of the mean. σ^2 = the variance of the continuously compounded rate of return on the share. So σ is the standard deviation of the continuously compounded return.

$$dist\ 1 = \frac{\ln(S/E) + (r + \tfrac{1}{2}\sigma^2)t}{\sigma\sqrt{t}}$$

$$dist\ 2 = dist\ 1 - \sigma\sqrt{t}$$

The above formulation is complex, and its derivation obviously involves mathematics beyond elementary levels. But since readers may be more interested in its application than its proof, a numerical example is appended. Assume that the current share price is £2.36, the strike price is £1.90 and there are twenty-two days of the option to run to expiration. With a risk-free rate of return of 9 per cent and a variance of return of 16 per cent (found by contrasting the performance of the company's shares against the market), we can now find the likely value of the option according to the Black and Scholes model.

From statistical tables, not published in this book, $N(dist\ 1)$ and $N(dist\ 2)$ can be found to be 0.990 and 0.987, respectively. The theoretical value of the option in pence can be found from the formula to be:

$$236 \times 0.990 - \frac{190 \times 0.987}{2.71828^{0.0925} \times 0.06027}$$

This simplifies to 47 pence. The answer can easily be checked in general terms. The value of the option must be at least the difference between the stock price and the exercise price, namely 46 pence. Since the option period is short, the option premium should be near to this figure.

Referring back to Figure 11.2, which shows the key variables in option pricing, what is most interesting is not the variables that are used in the formulations but those that were left out. It is important to note that in the above model no mention has been made of market direction or bias as an appropriate input. An implicit assumption of the model is that the market moves in a random fashion. In other words, while prices will change, the chances of a rise are the same as the chances of a fall, and the likelihood of large movements relative to small movements is normally distributed. Plotting daily market movements over time should, according to this assumption, result in the bell-shaped curve, the normal distribution.

Most banks nowadays use computer models based on their own formulations which draw on the above routine for pricing currency options. Some institutions use their own in-house formulae for valuing currency options, but these are similar to the Black and Scholes or Garman and Kohlhagen models.

Corporate use of currency options

If a company wishes to leave open the possibility of making a currency gain on a receivable or payable, while protecting itself against adverse movements in the exchange rate, it can do so via the currency option market. Currency options are of particular interest to the treasurer where a future currency cash flow is uncertain as in the case of putting in a contract tender, or issuing a foreign currency price list. In the case of a tender, if the contract is not awarded, the company merely lets the currency option lapse – or, if it pays to do otherwise, it sells it on at a profit. If the company obtains the contract tendered for it would exchange the currency option for a forward option running out to the payment dates under the contract.

Treasurers may also use currency options to hedge a contractually agreed deal to protect the downside exchange risk on a receivable or payable, while leaving open the upside potential. Currency options have become particularly attractive to corporate treasurers in times when there is substantial volatility in the foreign exchange markets. In 1984 the dollar was strengthening rapidly against most currencies, although many corporate treasurers felt that it was clearly overvalued in terms of purchasing power parity criteria. Given that trends in the market and purchasing power parity considerations pointed in opposite directions, it might have been an apposite time to use currency options. After the event, of course, it would have been better not to hedge dollar receivables at all, but this view only emerges with the benefit of hindsight.

A price has to be paid to secure the benefit of an option. This is the front-end non-returnable premium which the option writer receives whether or not the company exercises its option. The decision to use currency options needs to be carefully assessed taking into account the likelihood of the currency flow taking place, the volatility of the exchange rate until the funds are received and the cost of the premium. The answer to the criticism that some treasurers make to the effect that currency options are expensive, comes back loud and clear. Why not write options yourself, then?

Of course, one of the major problems with currency options traded on the Philadelphia, London or Amsterdam stock exchanges is that they have specific expiration dates which will usually differ from the date up to which cover is required. Because of this, there has developed an over-the-counter (OTC) market in which tailor-made options are bought and sold privately between banks and their customers. The growth of exchange traded and OTC currency options is really complementary. The exchange traded markets are used by banks hedging OTC positions. The OTC currency option business is made up largely of corporate activity. Increased volume in one market supports increased activity in the other. There are obvious reasons why a large volume of corporate currency option business has been channelled through the OTC rather than directly through exchange markets. First and foremost is the fact that OTC options are tailor-made to meet a company's specific needs. A company may therefore ask a bank to quote a price on a currency option which matches exactly its hedge requirements with respect to the currency to be bought and sold, the amount, the price and the time period to be covered. The option specifications of exchange traded products are standardized so that a company's precise needs will not easily be met through this marketplace.

Corporate treasurers are also attracted by the fact that OTC transactions are operationally straightforward and are rather similar to forward foreign exchange dealing procedures. It should be noted that there is no formal secondary market in OTC currency options which makes them less flexible than exchange traded options. The company can only sell its OTC option back to the bank writing it but OTC options have far greater flexibility for companies in terms of expiry dates, amounts involved and the possibility of dealing in currencies not quoted on the traded exchanges. Banks may be prepared to tailor options in a wider range of currencies than those quoted on the currency options markets. In Table 11.1 a comparison between exchange traded and OTC options is given.

An overview

Currency options provide the right, but not the obligation, to buy or sell a specific currency at a specific price at any time prior to a specified date. That options give a right but not an obligation means that commercial users of the market are able to obtain insurance against an adverse movement in the exchange rate while still retaining the opportunity to benefit from a favourable exchange movement. At the same time, the maximum risk

Table 11.1 Exchange traded and OTC options compared

	Exchange traded	OTC
Contact terms, including amounts	Standardized	Fixed to suit circumstances; terms are not standard
Expiration	Standardized	Determined by requirements of customers
Transaction method	Stock exchange type medium	Bank-to-client or bank-to-bank
Secondary market	Continuous secondaray market	No formal secondary market
Commissions	Negotiable	Negotiable but usually built into the premium
Participants	Exchange members and clients	Banks, corporations and financial institutions

to the buyer of an option is the actual cost of the front-end premium. Currency options have not been designed as a substitute for forward markets but as a new, distinct financial vehicle that offers significant opportunities and advantages to those seeking either protection or profit from changes in exchange rates.

Currency options come in two forms. There are traded currency options which are like traded options on shares and are for a standardized capital amount and have standardized delivery (maturity) dates. There are also over-the-counter options which are tailored by banks for their clients' individual requirements as to amount and maturity.

If a company wishes to leave open the possibility of making a currency gain on a receivable or payable while protecting itself against adverse movements in the exchange rate, it can do so via the currency option market. Currency options are of particular interest to the treasurer where a future currency cash flow is uncertain, as in the case of putting in a contract tender. If the contract is not awarded, the company merely lets the currency option lapse – or if it pays it to do otherwise, it sells it on at a profit. If the company obtains the contract tendered for, it would exchange the currency option for a series of forwards running out to the payment dates under the contract.

Treasurers may also use currency options to hedge a contractually agreed deal to protect the downside exchange risk on a receivable or payable, whilst leaving open the upside potential. Currency options have become particularly attractive to corporate treasurers in times when there is large volatility in the foreign exchange markets. Currency options also provide an easy way for a company to take positions and to speculate in foreign currency.

12

Interest rate risk

Interest rate risk is concerned with the sensitivity of profit, cash flows or valuation of the firm to changes in interest rates. Viewed from the perspective of this definition, the firm should analyse how its profit, cash outturns and value change in response to changes in interest rate levels. Should its profits and cash flows fall when interest rates rise, then the risk-averse company, seeking to stabilize profit trends, will finance itself with fixed rate funds. A speculative housebuilder might be a company falling into this category. However, some companies' profits and cash flows move directly with interest rates – this is true of many financial institutions. Such firms might, if they were risk averse, fund themselves with floating rate finance. Having said all this, firms may back their view of the market by funding themselves in a particular way. Thus the housebuilder who anticipates a fall in interest rates might source from floating rate funds. Interest rate exposure arises from two sources. There is macroeconomic exposure – the kind that the housebuilder in the example faced. And there is the exposure that the lender faces in respect of interest receivable on his deposit and, similarly, that the borrower faces relating to interest to be paid on loans drawn down.

We take interest rate risk further in this chapter – but first of all it is necessary to consider the term structure of interest rates because this topic is at the heart of most analysis in this area.

The term structure of interest rates

The term structure of interest rates can be thought of as a graph of interest rates on securities of a particular risk class at a particular time, in which the interest rate is plotted on the vertical axis and time to maturity on the horizontal axis. Term structure theory is concerned with why the term structure has a particular shape at a particular time. Analysts sometimes

108

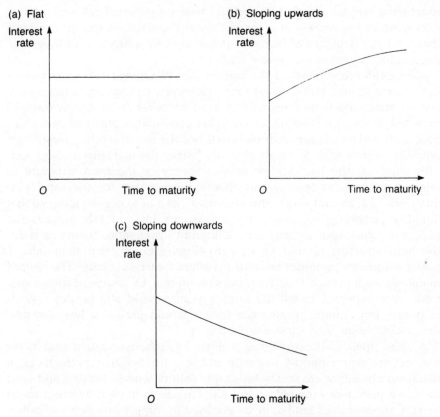

Figure 12.1 Types of term structure.

refer to the term structure as being flat (same interest for all maturities), upward-sloping (long-term interest rates higher than short-term interest rates), or downward-sloping (short-term interest rates higher than long-term rates). Figure 12.1 illustrates these three situations.

The best known explanation of the term structure is the expectations theory. According to this hypothesis, expectations of future interest rates constitute the key determinant of the yield/maturity relationship. Each investor can buy either long-term securities and hold them or buy short-term securities and continually reinvest in shorts at each maturity over the holding period. In equilibrium, the expected return for each holding period will tend to be the same, whatever alternative or combination of alternatives was chosen. As a result, the return on a long-term bond will tend to equal an unbiased average of the current short-term rates and future short-term rates expected to prevail to maturity of the long-term bond. With this background, one can calculate the implicit or expected short-term rate for any future period based upon actual rates of interest prevailing in the market at a specific time. Expectations theory contends that the term structure of interest rates is entirely a function of investors' expectations about future interest rates.

Most evidence underpins the importance of interest rate expectations in the term structure of interest rates. However, various economists have argued that long-term rates in fact tend to differ from the average of expected short-term rates because market participants prefer to lend short unless offered a premium sufficient to offset the risk of lending long. Such liquidity premia tend to be greater, the longer the maturity of the bond. This supports the liquidity preference theory of the term structure of interest rates. Advocates of this theory believe that for the most part investors wish to lend short, and organizations aim to borrow long, so that liquidity premiums are positive – that is, the forward rate exceeds the expected future spot interest rate. If liquidity preference theory is right, the term structure should be upward-sloping more often than not. A positive liquidity premium rewards investors for lending long. The reward manifests itself in high long-term rates of interest. Of course, if future spot rates were expected to fall the term structure could still be downward-sloping – but liquidity preference theory would predict a less dramatic downward slope than expectations theory.

A third theory, the preferred habitat hypothesis, argues that bond markets are segmented by maturity and that the maturity preferences of market participants are so strong that investors tend to borrow and lend only in a particular range of maturities. Therefore, in each different credit market, interest rates tend to be determined by supply and demand rather than by interest rate expectations. This explanation is sometimes called the market segmentation theory, or the hedging pressure theory.

Finally, there is the inflation premium theory. Like the liquidity preference explanation, this theory argues that long-term interest rates reflect investors' expectations about future short-term interest rates plus a premium for risk. However, advocates of the theory contend that the principal source of risk is the rate of inflation. They argue that investors are interested in real returns and that the primary determinant in the term structure of interest rates is investors' expectations of inflation over different holding periods, which is the critical factor by which investors translate nominal interest rates into real expected returns.

Whichever theory of term structure seems to predominate in the domestic market should hold for the Euromarket. In the absence of capital controls, arbitrage would ensure that virtual equality of internal and external rates at each maturity, and whatever holds for the domestic market would also hold for Eurorates. In other words, there is normally no independent Eurodollar term structure of interest rates.

If capital controls are in place and they affect all maturities equally, the internal term structure might not be identical to the external one, but since Eurorates should tend to be at the same position relative to internal rates for each maturity, a nearly identical term structure should hold. As in the domestic market, if Eurocurrency investors think interest rates will drop, they will try to lock into long-term deposits; this will tend to lower the long-term yield to maturity.

The term structure of Eurocurrency interest rates will be consonant with the market's interest rate forecasts if, and only if, the yield on a long-term deposit equals the expected yield obtained from investing in short-term securities and reinvesting the proceeds successively in short-term deposits at the interest rate expected to prevail during each future period.

The above point can be observed easily be reference to a numerical example. Assume that a firm has money to invest for, say, six months. It might invest now for the whole six-month period. Or it might invest now for only three months and then reinvest for a further three later on. Clearly, if the interest is for six months now, the firm will receive a quotation for a fixed rate for the whole six-month period with interest being credited at the end of the period. Also, if the firm invests for three months expecting to extend the investment by reinvesting at the end of that period for a further three months, it can expect to receive an offer of a fixed rate for three months with interest credited at the end of the period. But the firm could also obtain a forward/forward fixed interest rate for the period from the beginning of month four to the end of month six. By pursuing this latter policy, the firm would have manufactured exactly the same investment as locking in for the whole six months – so the proceeds should, in present value terms, be the same. After all the two investments are exactly equal in terms of risk, so they should yield the same returns.

If the firm invests for six months in accordance with the first scenario above, the proceeds of investing £1 now will be:

$$£1\left[1 + r_6\left(\frac{6}{12}\right)\right]$$

where r_6 is the annual (as bankers quote it) interest rate for six months. Investing according to the second scenario, the terminal proceeds of investing £1 now would be:

$$£1\left[1 + r_3\left(\frac{3}{12}\right)\right]\left[1 + r_{3/6}\left(\frac{3}{12}\right)\right]$$

where r_3 is the annual interest rate for the first three months and $r_{3/6}$ is the annual interest rate from the beginning of month four to the end of month six.

Generalizing from the first equation, we could say that the terminal proceeds for the former scenario amounted to:

$$1 + \left(r_{t_2} \times \frac{t_2}{12} \right)$$

where r is the interest rate and t_2 is the far term in months. Similarly, the terminal value of the latter scenario can be said to be equal to:

$$\left[1 + \left(r_{t_1} \times \frac{t_1}{12} \right) \right] \left[1 + \left(r_{t_{1-2}} \times \frac{t_{1 \to 2}}{12} \right) \right]$$

where t_1 is the near term in months and $t_{1 \to 2}$ is the difference between the near and far term in months.

Since the proceeds from the two investments should be the same, it follows logically that:

$$\frac{1 + \left(r_{t_2} \times \frac{t_2}{12} \right)}{1 + \left(r_{t_1} \times \frac{t_1}{12} \right)} = 1 + r_{t_1 \to 2}$$

The figure obtained from the above expression for $r_{t1 \to 2}$ may be annualized to put it into terms used by bankers.

This forward rate is, of course, essentially the market's best estimate of a future interest rate based upon the term structure of interest rates, from which both forward quotes of interest rates are derived. An understanding of these very basic ideas is useful because it is the underpinning of various quotations to do with interest rates – for example FRAs and some other instruments which we now address in this chapter.

Forward rate agreements

Forward rate agreements (FRAs) allow borrowers or investors to lock in today a LIBOR rate accruing from a forward start date for a given period, for example for month 3 in the future to month 6. The FRA is currently an off-balance-sheet instrument. It is widely used to cover short-term interest rate exposures for periods up to two or three years. It is a contract between two parties to agree an interest rate on a notional loan or deposit of a specified amount and maturity at a specific future date and to make payments between counterparties computed by reference to changes in the interest rate. FRAs involve no exchange of the principal amount. They are concerned only with the interest element. To hedge an interest rate exposure, the notional amount of the FRA contract is made equal to the principal amount of the underlying asset or liability.

A borrower desirous of hedging an interest rate exposure in three months' time for a period of three months would purchase a three-months FRA starting in three months. This is known as purchasing a '3s versus 6s' FRA (or 'threes' against 'sixes'). An investor with floating rate assets wishing to lock in an investment rate for a similar period would sell an FRA contract. To show how FRAs work, assume that a borrower has a one-year floating rate loan which has to be rolled over every three months based on three months' LIBOR (London interbank offer rate – the rate at which banks offer money to each other in the London money markets). For the first three months, LIBOR has already been fixed. The borrower is concerned about a short-term increase in interest rates and wishes to hedge this exposure for the following three months. This can be achieved by purchasing an FRA in respect of the next interest paid and for a notional amount identical to the underlying loan transaction.

In three months' time, the borrower continues to borrow from the original source of finance. The FRA contract which he has entered into will have the same start date as the next interest rate repricing date. On that day, the three-month LIBOR rate is compared with the rate agreed under the FRA contract. If the FRA rate is greater than LIBOR, then the borrower will pay the seller of the FRA contract the difference between the two rates. The borrower's cost of borrowing will be equal to the market LIBOR rate plus the difference paid to the FRA as counterparty. The all-in rate will be the same as the rate agreed under the FRA contract. If the FRA rate is less than LIBOR, then the FRA counterparty will pay the borrower the difference between the two rates. This time the cost of borrowing will be the three-month LIBOR rate less the difference received from the FRA counterparty. Similarly, the net cost to the borrower will be the same rate as agreed under the FRA contract.

In the FRA market it is common practice to discount the net interest amount and settle at the beginning of an interest period. The discount factor used is the prevailing LIBOR rate. By dealing an FRA contract the borrower can fix his borrowing costs for, say, the next six months. Should he wish, he can fix his borrowing cost for the rest of the year by purchasing a strip of FRAs – a borrower will not only purchase a '3s versus 6s' but also a '6s versus 9s' and a '9s versus 12s' contract.

As an example, assume that a corporate borrower deals a US$10m 3s × 6s FRA on 10 September 1989 for settlement on 10 December 1989 based on a maturity date of 10 March 1990. The contract rate is 9.65 per cent and the contract period is 90 days. If, on 10 December 1989, the three-month

LIBOR fixing is at 10⅛ per cent, the settlement amount payable on that date would be:

$$\frac{(0.10125 - 0.0965) \times 10,000,000 \times 90/360}{1 + (0.10125 \times 90/360)}$$

= $11,581.83 payable to the buyer of the FRA.

The above settlement formula is virtually standard in the business nowadays.

The price of each FRA contract is a function of the yield curve. It will be priced in the manner explained by reference to forward interest rates in the section in this chapter on the term structure of interest rates.

Interest rate futures

Chapter 10, on financial futures, explained how futures contracts could be used to hedge currency exposures. They can also be used to hedge interest rate exposures. Like currency futures, interest rate futures are traded on exchanges and are standardized. Such standardized features include a set contract size, a specific settlement date and a specific interest rate and period. These standard features make them less than utterly appealing to corporations as hedging tools because they do not allow for specific exposures. FRAs are probably more convenient hedging tools for companies. However, interest rate futures are widely used by banks and financial institutions for hedging their portfolios. These institutions are not generally concerned with matching, with 100 per cent exactitude, their underlying exposures.

As we have mentioned earlier, financial futures contracts are for standardized amounts and delivery dates. The number of instruments traded is limited and they are traded off balance sheet. All futures contracts are registered with the clearing house which becomes the counterparty to any deal, and there are obligatory initial and variation margin requirements for all futures contracts.

Interest rate swaps

Interest rate swaps provide another means of eliminating interest rate exposure. Swaps were the topic of Chapter 9 of this book, where they were dealt with extensively. To spend more time on them here would be repetitious.

Interest rate options

Interest rate options include caps, floors and collars – their mechanism, theory, advantages and disadvantages are just like currency options which were discussed in Chapter 11.

Swaps, futures and FRAs lock in an interest rate. The company is protected against any adverse movements of interest rates, but it cannot take advantage of favourable movements of interest rates.

Interest rate options overcome this. They provide the right but not the obligation to fix a rate of interest, on a notional loan or deposit, for an agreed amount, for a fixed term, on a specific forward date. The buyer of the option has the right but not the obligation to deal at the agreed rate. He is protected against adverse rate movements but is able to take advantage of a favourable movement in interest rates. The seller guarantees an interest rate if the option is exercised. He receives a fee – the premium – for providing this guarantee. The factors which determine the price of interest rate options are similar to those that determine currency option prices – remember Black and Scholes, volatilities, and so on. If not, refer again to Chapter 11.

The most common type of interest rate option available to borrowers as a hedge against rising interest rates is the interest rate cap. Interest rate floors protect investors against falling interest rates.

An interest rate cap is an arrangement where, in return for a premium, the seller of the cap undertakes, over an agreed period, to compensate the buyer of the cap whenever a reference interest rate (for example three or six months' LIBOR) exceeds a pre-agreed maximum interest rate (the cap rate). In addition to having this protection whenever the reference rate exceeds the cap rate, the buyer of the cap can benefit when the reference rate is below the cap rate. This is because, at such times, the borrower is not locked into a fixed rate and can take advantage of the lower market rates.

If an investor purchases a floor he will be compensated by the seller whenever, say, three months' LIBOR falls below a pre-agreed minimum rate. The buyer will exercise his option only if rates fall below the agreed level and he is therefore able to enjoy the benefits if interest rates remain at levels above the agreed rate.

Interest settlement procedures for a cap or floor transaction are straightforward. A borrower is compensated by the seller of the cap whenever the reference rate exceeds the cap rate. A floor investor is compensated whenever the reference rate falls below the floor rate.

There are such things as zero cost options for both currencies and interest rates – for the latter they are termed collars. Effectively, the simultaneous purchase and sale of a cap and a floor is known as a 'collar'. In order to illustrate how collars work, assume that the treasurer wishes to protect his interest income by buying a floor struck at 10 per cent. But he does not wish to pay the full premium and therefore sells a cap struck at, for example, 13 per cent. In this case, the cost of buying the floor exactly matches the premium received from selling the cap, so we have a zero cost collar. By undertaking these transactions, the company has an investment which pays a minimum of 10 per cent if the floating rate is at or below 10 per cent and a maximum of 13 per cent when the floating rate is at or above 13 per cent on the interest determination date. If the floating rate is between 10 per cent and 13 per cent, then the return equals the reference rate.

Dealing an interest rate collar is always cheaper than buying the straight interest rate cap or floor since the buyer is giving up some of his upside benefit if rates move in his favour. This is exactly synonymous to the zero cost currency option.

An overview

Interest rate risk is concerned with the sensitivity of profit, cash flows or valuation of the firm to changes in interest rates. Choices between fixed and floating rate funding flow from careful analysis of a firm's interest rate exposure and a view of future rate movements. There are a number of financial instruments by which the firm may manage its interest rate exposure. FRAs, interest rate futures and interest rate swaps may all be used to lock in on interest rates for the firm. With them, the company may be protected against any adverse movement of interest rates but it cannot take advantage of favourable movements. Interest rate options overcome this. They provide the right but not the obligation to fix a rate of interest on a notional loan or deposit, for an agreed amount, for a fixed term, on a specific forward date. Caps, collars and floors are all examples of interest rate options and their pricing derives from the Black and Scholes techniques discussed earlier.

13

The value of growth options

The route towards the identification of the expected profitability of an investment project is well known to top managers in most enterprises. In the usual discounted cash flow (DCF) calculations, the project's anticipated cash flows are viewed as one of the early ports of call in terms of developing relevant data for appraisal purposes. To be sure, sensitivity analysis is available to sophisticate the appraisal – this might involve looking at outturns with lower sales projections or higher cost levels or different timing of sales penetration and so on. But, for a broad spectrum of projects, there is a complexity which renders the traditional discounting methodology less than wholly appropriate. This chapter focuses upon that problem. If does not conclude that the typical model cannot be adapted to meet the situation. It can and it is not too difficult.

The angle that is so often taken in investment appraisal is a static one. It is static in the sense that operating decisions are viewed as being fixed in advance and, as such, give rise to the base case set of incremental cash flows. It is this feature that is at the heart of why the pure discounted cash flow techniques, as used by so many companies, may be less than perfect in simulating the business world.

In reality, good managers are frequently good because they pursue policies that maintain flexibility on as many fronts as possible and they maintain options that promise upside potential. In respect of investment decision making, this means keeping open the opportunity to make decisions contingent upon information which may become available in the future. For example, dependent upon actual levels of demand or of competition or of cost, the rate of output of a new product may be accelerated, existing facilities may be extended or, should outturns be less attractive than expected, they may be closed temporarily or even abandoned altogether.

Research and development is an obvious case in point. Testing out a new market via a pilot plant is clearly another. Oil exploration obviously falls into this category, levels of exploration and investment being highly contingent upon oil prices prevailing. And mining and quarrying are similar kinds of investment – extraction or temporary closure or even abandonment being obvious courses of action which will be a function of actual prices of and/or demand for the product concerned. International investment is another example. Invariably it begins with a small commitment which may be scaled upwards should the environment prove profitable, or it may be curtailed should the host country appear to offer less attractive cash flows than anticipated. And, of course, many purely domestic investments are rather like this, having scale-up possibilities.

All of these examples have one key feature in common – the firm has flexibility in terms of its course of action depending upon outcomes and factors unknown at the time of the project's inception. Qualitatively, the idea is fairly straightforward. And we can take it further by incorporating numerical data.

An example using decision trees

Let us look at an example; it makes explanation easier. Consider a decision facing a minerals exploration company. It concerns a silver mine with a residual of two million troy ounces of silver which could all be extracted next year assuming a sufficiently attractive price – but the exploration company has a concession which lasts only until next year. Assume that the current price is 205 pence per ounce, having moved up from 180. The best estimate of next year's price is put at 200 pence which, with variable costs of 180 pence, would yield a contribution (and profit – since, at least for this example, fixed costs are put at zero) of 20 pence per ounce. Re-opening the mine would involve a one-off cost of £450,000. Assuming that 12 per cent per annum is the appropriate discount rate for the project, it can be seen that the traditional discounted cash flow approach shows it to be a no-go decision. The numbers, summarized in Table 13.1, indicate a negative net present value (NPV) of some £94,000. Does this mean that the mine is worthless? Traditional DCF analysis based on best estimates seems to point in this direction.

But this classic discounted cash flow appraisal is not good enough. It ignores the options to mine if the price is high enough or not to mine if the price is not sufficiently attractive to do so. Assume that the best estimate price of 200 pence per ounce has been arrived at as a mid-point of estimates of 250 pence and 150 pence per ounce – each of these possible prices has a 50 per cent probability factor associated with it. Remember that variable costs of extraction were put at 180 pence per ounce. Clearly, should a price of only 150 pence be available in the marketplace, there is no logical way that a profit-orientated company would extract any silver. It would leave the mineral in the ground. At a price of 250 pence, things are obviously very different. The interesting thing is that including an allowance for the possibility of not going ahead with extraction, the project has a positive net present value on the basis of expected monetary value analysis – simply multiplying anticipated cash flows by their associated

Table 13.1 Silver mine projections – base case

		Year
	0	1
Re-opening costs	−£450,000	
Contribution – silver sales		+£400,000
Discount factor at 12%	1.00	0.89
Present value	−£450,000	+£356,000
Net present value	−£94,000	

Time (year)   0   1

Event Silver price 250p/ounce	Probability 0.5	Implication Mine	Net cash inflow 70p × 2 million = £1.4m

MINE

INVEST
£450,000

DO NOT MINE

Event Silver price 150p/ounce	Probability 0.5	Implication Do not mine	Net cash inflow £0

$$\text{Net present value at 12\%} = -\pounds450,000 + \frac{(1,400,000 \times 0.5) + (0 \times 0.5)}{1.12}$$

$$= -\pounds450,000 + \pounds625,000$$

$$= +\pounds175,000$$

Figure 13.1 Silver mine projections accounting for option not to extract metal.

probability and then discounting. Figure 13.1 indicates that the expected net present value on this basis is £175,000. The mine is certainly not worthless.

It has to be conceded that the above example is simplistic. However, it does lead us to some undeniable conclusions. The difference between the bottom lines in Table 13.1 and Figure 13.1 arises because the latter takes cognizance of the option not to mine should the price fail to yield a contribution when the time to consider extraction arrives. In other words, the classic, single outturn, non-option-orientated analysis ignores the tactical flexibility which every good manager tries to keep open. DCF analysis has a lot to offer, but it somehow fails to reflect adequately the reality of the world of business.

Flexibility and value creation

What should be clear is that the ability to change tactical direction in response to new information can contribute significant increments to value. And such financial flexibility should be given due weight at the gestation phase of a project's life – that is, at the quantitative appraisal stage. Investments which possess this flexibility have the characteristics of options. An option gives the holder a right but not an obligation to do something (usually to buy or sell at an agreed price). Research and development gives the firm the right but not the obligation to scale up from the pilot plant to the full commercial scale. Oil exploration rights, or possession of mining reserves, give the firm the opportunity to extract (which may or may not be a right, for example, because of planning consents) but not the obligation to so do. Expansion into a foreign territory gives the firm the possibility (again it may not be a right) of scaling up should things turn out attractively, but to abandon should outturns be less positive.

These kinds of investments readily equate to options in stock market terms – and should therefore be valued accordingly. Stock market options give the holder the right to acquire or sell securities at a particular price (the strike price) within a specified timeframe but there is not an obligation to do so. In the case of certain kinds of investment project, the firm acquires an opportunity (not necessarily a right) to do something but is not committed. The similarity is obvious.

A call option in the stock market gives the holder the right to buy shares at a fixed price over a period of time but not the obligation to do so. Similarly, an investment in research and development gives the firm the potential to acquire the benefits thereof for the cost of commercialization. The owner of a mine or oil well has the possibility of acquiring the proceeds from the mine's or oil well's output but does not have an obligation to do so and, like the stock market call option buyer, he or she may defer selling the proceeds of the asset's output. Pre-emptive (and not necessarily heavy) investment in new markets, whether domestic or international, may give the firm the edge when it comes to opportunities for scaling up to a full-sized production and distribution network while retaining the option to withdraw from that market if outturns are unfavourable. With respect to research and development, minerals extraction projects and exploratory investments in new markets, including international ones, classic DCF techniques, unless accompanied by serious modification, fail to take into account the tactical flexibility and value-creating upside potential of subsequent add-on aspects and consequently understate true investment potential.

Various articles have appeared stressing the need to extend the analysis of certain kinds of investment decisions to embrace these option-type characteristics. Reference to the put option aspect of capital investment – the value of the potential to abandon the project – has a long history. The option to expand further – the call option – has been the focus of a number of papers, which apply the option pricing model to mining and oil exploration projects, minerals industries and pharmaceutical research and development and international investment.

The message is that the old-style capital appraisal techniques are more than adequate in terms of dealing with pure cash-saving investments but leave something to be desired where there is operational flexibility or contingent opportunities for growth. In these circumstances, DCF methods consistently undervalue projects due to their failure to allow for strategic flexibility. At the current time it is fair to say that far too few standard textbooks on financial management give this topic sufficient coverage. When it is incorporated, it is frequently referred to by the letters PVGO – present value of growth opportunities.

Dixit and Pindyck (*Investment under Uncertainty*, Princeton University Press, 1994), in their development of a logic of option-based strategies, point out that 'the ability to delay an irreversible investment expenditure can profoundly affect the decision to invest. It also undermines the simple net present value rule, and hence the theoretical foundation of standard neoclassical investment models'. They go on to conclude that 'as a result the NPV rule . . . must be modified'.

The Black and Scholes model

It is the firm view of this chapter that a means of appraisal which incorporates a base case DCF calculation plus an option valuation routine makes it ideal for analysing, for example, extractive industry investments, research and development projects, investments in markets with growth potential and international expansion. The basic framework can be sophisticated without too much difficulty to give it the full range of Black and Scholes features – see Chapter 11. But one of the key assumptions of the Black and Scholes model, the standard financial method for valuing options, is that the security price concerned fluctuates in a random fashion and the variance of the return on the security is constant over the life of the option.

In the cases of mining projects and oil exploration, it is usual that the price of the commodity (and hence returns) is likely to fluctuate in a random fashion, making application of the Black and Scholes methodology appropriate. This is rarely true with research and development projects or investments with growth opportunities or international investment either (except mining, oil, commodities and the like). Potential returns may be vastly skewed. In such circumstances it may be entirely inappropriate to use a Black and Scholes-based method since one of its key assumptions is that prices follow a random walk with constant variance over the life of the option.

In cases where the distribution of returns is non-normal, valuation of growth options might involve a decision tree route. Calculation of the base case (that is without the inclusion of growth options) net present value normally comes first. If this is itself positive, the project clearly gets a green light. Even if it is negative, it can give management an idea of the necessary magnitude of PVGO in order to make the project financially viable. This value might then be estimated by decision tree techniques or the project may merely be sanctioned somewhat intuitively. For example, should a $20m project for a motor company promise a net present value of minus $0.25m in respect of investment in vehicles in China with no PVGO built in, the management might conclude that achieving a further $¼m net present value from future follow-on investment should prove a relatively small problem and proceed with the investment.

Another example with decision trees

The key question that must always be asked in choosing a methodology for valuing real operating options concerns whether the Black and Scholes model's assumptions are applicable in the case being examined. The less applicable they are, the more certain we should be about using valuation techniques based on decision tree analysis.

Let us look at a simple example of a situation with substantial growth opportunities which include the scaling-up of a project should outturns be sufficiently attractive. The base case cash flow scenario, without any real operating option considerations included, is as follows. The project is expected to involve a net cash investment in year zero of £24m. In future years, the best estimate of net tax cash inflows is put at £1m in the first year, rising to £3m in the second year, followed by inflows of £4m each for the third year to the twelfth inclusive. Assume that the appropriate discount rate is 10 per cent per annum. With this background, the project's net present value comes out at £0.2m negative. The position is summarized in Table 13.2.

Table 13.2 Valuing growth opportunities

Year	0	1	2	3 → 12
Base case				
Best estimate cash flows (£m)	−24	+1	+3	+4 p.a.
Present value at 10% (£m)	−24	+0.9	+2.5	+20.4
Net present value	£0.2m (negative)			
The operating option				
But if best estimate cash flows are underpinned by these subjective probability forecasts (£m and probability)		+2(0.2)	+5(0.2)	+12(0.05)
		+1(0.6)	+3(0.6)	+8(0.1)
		+0(0.2)	+1(0.2)	+4(0.6)
				+1(0.2)
				+0(0.05)
And if year 3 flows reach £12m, scale-up occurs, then		Year	4	5 → 12
Additional cash flows over and above the base case would be (£m)			−40	+25 p.a.
Net present value of scale-up (at time zero) would be	£63.41m			
With a probability of	0.05			
Giving an expected monetary value to scale-up scenario of	£3.17m			
Overall net present value of base case plus scale-up opportunity (approx.)	£3m			

But assume that the best estimates reflect a range of views of managers. In other words, these estimates are derived from managers' expectations using their own probabilities of outturns. Assume also that these suggest that the best estimate cash flow for year one of £1m is based upon a 20 per cent probability of £2m occurring, a 60 per cent probability of £1m and a 20 per cent probability attached to a flow of zero. In year two, the best estimate of cash flow of £3m is based on a 20 per cent probability of £5m, a 20 per cent probability of £1m and a 60 per cent probability of £3m. And, for years three to twelve, the estimate of £4m is underpinned by probabilities of 5 per cent attaching to both outturns of £12m and zero, an expectation of 10 per cent attaching to £8m, an expectation of 60 per cent attaching to £4m and an expectation of 20 per cent attaching to £1m. Assume further that if the £12m outturn is achieved in year three, the firm would spend an additional £30m in expansion investment in year four and this would give rise to additional net inflows of £25m for each of years five to twelve inclusive. Of course, given that the £12m inflow in year three attracts only a 5 per cent probability, so the scale-up scenario attracts only a similar 1 in 20 expectation. However, as can be seen in the bottom half of Table 13.2, the expected value of the scale-up has an expected monetary value (based on an NPV of £63.41m and a probability of 0.05) of £3.17m.

In effect it can be seen that the project, looked at in terms of best estimate cash flows, has an overall negative value of £0.2m. But allowing for possible growth and its corollary in scaling-up, the project has a bottom line positive value of around £3m. Of course, the above scenario, summarized in Table 13.2, is simplistic. The cash inflows after the scale-up would have probabilities attached to them too and there may be further scaling up after year four. But the intention of the illustration is to make the point that merely restricting financial analysis to most likely outturns, when there are growth opportunities about, is not necessarily an approach that is likely to yield relevant information for optimum investment decisions. Without a perspective which incorporates operating flexibility, the long-run goal of a firm's management in terms of seeking a portfolio of projects which maximizes value in the long term is unlikely to be achieved. Failure to look beyond best estimate cash flow considerations actually penalizes projects with growth opportunities, the very projects that the firm needs in its pursuit of long-term success.

Of course, to take cognizance of this feature of strategic investment decisions might involve the sort of analysis set out in Table 13.2, or it might encompass the sort of generalized approach in the example of the motor company expanding into China – see the end of the immediately previous section of this chapter. Or it might involve calculation of the base case value plus a somewhat intuitive statement that the expected monetary value of growth opportunities is likely to be worth, for example, £2m. However, it has to be admitted that this last approach is altogether open to a greater degree of biasing – always a problem in real-world forecasting – than the former two approaches.

An overview

The valuation of projects that, potentially, have more than one tranche of investment, with the latter a function of the former, or of market conditions, requires a form of investment appraisal which is beyond traditional discounted cash flow – it needs to take account of available options that the firm might pursue. What we need to look at is, effectively, the base case value which would be the product of traditional DCF analysis and, on top of this, the value of the discretion associated with either undertaking or not undertaking the follow-on scenario. One of the strategies that adds corporate value is to maintain flexibility through structuring investments – and indeed a whole host of other managerial actions – in a manner paralleling options. Investments of this kind should be:

1. Evaluated to embrace the option characteristics.
2. Analysed from a standpoint beyond the traditional DCF model.

Structuring investment decisions in such a way as to confer an option element enhances shareholder value over and above the base case present value scenario. Failure to evaluate investments of this kind to allow for this option aspect can only result in an understatement of potential shareholder value created.

14

Is the international investment decision different?

Analysing capital investment decisions involves comparing cash inflows with cash outflows from a project. Investment appraisal systems are frequently collectively termed capital budgeting, and this focuses upon expected incremental cash flows associated with a project. The specification of these flows for the overseas project creates the usual difficulties found in a domestic capital project, but international project analysis is much more complex. Although the basic pattern follows the same model as that suggested by corporate financial theory, the multinational firm must consider factors peculiar to international operations.

A project may be estimated to produce considerable cash flows in a foreign territory but, because of exchange control restrictions, the bulk of these foreign cash flows may not be distributable to the parent company. In these circumstances, looking at the project purely in terms of cash flows accruing in the foreign territory may indicate that it is worth investing. Is this good enough? Surely the present value to the parent company is a function of future cash flows accruing to it which are distributable to the parent company's investors. But we stated that for the project concerned, the bulk of foreign territory cash flows were blocked by exchange controls. Surely it is only incremental cash flows which are remittable back to the parent company which add value for its shareholders? This means that our capital project might be looked at from at least two standpoints: incremental project cash flows and incremental parent cash flows. To the international company, though, it is only incremental parent cash flows that matter.

The international complications

There are six key categories of complexity in international capital budgeting about which analysts are advised to beware. These embrace situations where:

1. Full remittance of cash flows arising from a project are restricted in terms of payment to the parent.

2. Part of the parent input is via equipment.

3. Exchange rates are not expected to be constant throughout the project's life.

4. Different rates of tax apply in the country of the project and in the parent's country.

5. Royalties and management fees are involved.

6. There are knock-on effects impinging upon operations in the group elsewhere in the world.

We now consider each of these complexities in turn.

Remittance constraints on cash flows

In international capital budgeting a significant difference may exist between the cash generation of a project and the amount that is remittable to the parent. The main reason for this is the existence of exchange controls in the host nation. Management in an overseas subsidiary can be excused for focusing only upon project cash flows accruing locally. Overseas managers often ignore the consequences of an investment upon the rest of the corporation, and in particular the impact of the project at the level of distributable cash flows of the parent company. For the project, the appropriate incremental cash inflows are those additional cash outturns resulting from new operations after adjustment for local corporate taxes. From the parent's view, the critical incremental cash flow figures are the additional remittable funds to the parent treasury in London, New York or wherever. From the central treasury's point of view, the important cash flows relating to a new investment are incremental cash flows that are distributable to the multinational's shareholders. This means that management fees (net of the costs of providing supervision), royalties, interest, dividend remittances, loan inputs and repayments and equity inputs are all key cash flows.

According to corporate financial theory, the value of a project is determined by the net present value of future cash flows available for the investor. The parent multinational corporation should therefore value only those cash flows that are available for repatriation. This should be done net of any transfer costs, since it is only these remaining funds that can be used to pay corporate interest and dividends: it is only these funds that represent free cash flow. The estimation of parent cash flows involves focusing upon incremental remittable cash flows; whether they are actually remitted or not is immaterial, what is important is that they *may* be remitted.

In some countries, namely those without exchange controls, project cash flows may readily translate into parent cash flows. In other countries, international project evaluation should involve two key stages of analysis. First, project cash flows should be computed from the overseas subsidiary's standpoint, as if it were a separate free-standing entity. Focus, in the second stage of analysis, moves to the parent. Here analysis requires forecasts of the amounts and timing of distributable cash flows. It also requires information about taxes payable. In summary, then, it is distributable parent cash flows which matter.

For an overseas investment in a country where there are no restrictions on remittance, incremental cash flows accruing to the multinational corporation need to be forecast in local currency and then converted into the multinational corporation's home currency in accordance with expected exchange rates prevailing when such cash flows accrue. If, when subjected to home territory tax rules (which is the harshest tax treatment) the project still looks attractive then a clear green light is indicated.

Where a project is in a country from which cash flow repatriation is restricted, the relevant focus should be upon remittable incremental parent cash flows. Analysis might embrace the cash flows set out in Figure 14.1.

There are various means at the disposal of the group treasurer in order to unlock blocked overseas cash flows: such techniques as countertrade and barter are the most obvious. In overseas project evaluation, it is perfectly permissible to take credit as a parent flow for blocked cash generation to the extent that it can be unlocked by such means as to countertrade, etc., subject to costs of unblocking.

Equipment input to a project

The second major complication in international capital budgeting arises in situations in which the home-based company puts up part of its equity or loan capital in an overseas subsidiary by way of equipment or inventory. Clearly, the project should be debited with this input for the purpose of calculating project returns but, since it is parent returns that are of paramount importance, how should we treat this factor at the level of parent incremental cash flows?

The home territory company has surrendered value (in the form of equipment or inventory) in the expectation of obtaining greater value later on in terms of remittable, incremental parent cash flows. The problem that the financial analyst has is to put a value on the equipment or inventory surrendered. There is an ideally suited technique for valuing the property put in by the home territory company and this involves the use of the concept of deprival value. This has been defined by Bonbright, the

- Equity put in to overseas project
- Dividends back from overseas project.
- Equity capital remitted back to parent.
- Loans put in to overseas project.
- Loan interest back from overseas.
- Management fees, etc. received from overseas project net of supervision costs.
- Royalties.
- Equipment or inventory contributions to overseas project (here the opportunity cost is the relevant figures).
- Contribution accruing to the parent or to a subsidiary in a country where repatriation of funds is not restricted (or to other subsidiaries when repatriation is possible) on incremental sales to the project.
- Appropriate tax effect on remittance.
- The value of growth options (see Chapter 13)

Figure 14.1 Parent cash flows.

originator of the concept, in his book *The Valuation of Property*, as the 'adverse value of the entire loss, direct or indirect, that the owner might expect to suffer if he were to be deprived of the property'. In effect, in subscribing equipment or inventory, the home-territory company is voluntarily being deprived of assets in favour of the foreign business.

Bonbright advances three meaningful bases for valuation of an asset. These are:

1. The current purchase price of an asset in a comparable state of wear and tear: this is replacement cost (*RC*).
2. The net realizable value (*NRV*) of the asset: this is the current net disposable value.
3. The present value of the expected future earnings stream flowing from the asset (*PV*).

The Bonbright approach seems the relevant and logical way to assess the value forgone by the home-territory company in surrendering assets to an overseas venture. The correct basis of valuation is summarized in Figure 14.2.

Obviously when an asset subscribed to an overseas venture is completely unnecessary to the home operations, then the relevant valuation basis would be *NRV*. After all, the home company has forgone the opportunity to sell the asset for its realizable value.

Circumstances	Correct basis
NRV > PV > RC	RC
NRV > RC > PV	RC
PV > RC > NRV	RC
PV > NRV > RC	RC
RC > PV > NRV	PV
RC > NRV > PV	NRV

Figure 14.2 Basis of asset valuation.

Having identified the appropriate valuation method in respect of the asset subscribed to an overseas project, this becomes the initial minus item in the parent cash flow projections against which subsequent estimated inflows are set.

It is worth noting that, whether in a domestic or international situation, were one company to subscribe equipment and inventory to another company in return for a share of its equity, deprival value would provide the correct basis for valuing the input as part of the process of investment appraisal.

More detail on this topic – and indeed on the whole subject area of overseas capital budgeting – is available in *Multinational Finance* by Adrian Buckley (Prentice Hall, 1996).

Exchange rates

We now turn to the third area of complication: exchange rates. If exchange rates are in equilibrium at the time the project commences and if future exchange rates move in line with purchasing power parity and if, further, project cash inflows and outflows move in line with general inflation in the overseas territory, then, assuming that there are no exchange control restrictions and assuming that host territory and home country taxes are at similar rates, project cash flow analysis will give exactly the same indication about investment viability as parent cash flow analysis. Rarely, if ever, will all of these conditions hold.

Consequently it is recommended that estimated future project cash flows (net of local tax) be shown in money terms (that is, gross of expected host country inflation) and the project net present value should be calculated following the application of a money terms host country discount rate. Parent cash flows should be estimated by applying the expected future exchange rate to host country net cash flows if there are no exchange controls, or remittable net cash flows if exchange controls are in place or where they are expected to be introduced. Due allowance must be made for host and home country taxation impacts and a parent net present value would be estimated following the application of a risk-adjusted parent discount rate.

Estimation of future exchange rates might follow from projections of inflation rates, with corrections arising through purchasing power parity. Of course, it must be remembered that while purchasing power parity is found empirically to hold in the long term, movements in exchange rates often follow discontinuous paths with governments supporting currencies for long periods before giving in and letting the economics of inflation rate differentials have their full effect. Given that exchange rate movements are discontinuous, wise analysts may wish to reflect this in their forecasts – although the timing of when purchasing power parity is likely to reassert itself is incredibly difficult to predict. Perhaps this problem is best handled via sensitivity analysis with various sets of figures being prepared for different timings of purchasing power parity asserting itself.

Taxation

The fourth area of complication concerns taxation. Clearly, project cash flows should be estimated net of local taxation and parent cash flows should be calculated net of parent taxation.

Royalties and management fees

If royalties and management fees are charged by a home-based company to an overseas operating subsidiary, then these should be shown as a debit to the project cash flow and as a credit in the parent cash flow analysis. Strictly speaking, of course, income to be forgone and/or incremental costs to be incurred in deploying management in pursuit of the project should be set against parent cash inflows.

Impact elsewhere in the group

The final problem area in overseas capital budgeting involves investment projects where there are substantial knock-on effects on operations elsewhere within the group. For example, a motor manufacturer contemplating the establishment of a plant in Spain may find that the proposed investment will affect the operations of other units within the multinational group. This may arise, in part, through the new project's effect on sales of other parts of the multinational in Europe (for example, sales deriving from the French and German plants). But it may also arise through vertical integration by, for example, affecting the output of a mining operation in South America which is owned by the multinational corporation. It could be the case that the new plant is expected to absorb output from the mine. Where such knock-on effects exist, the firm needs to evaluate the project by aggregating all incremental cash flows accruing. Thus while cash flows in Spain are clearly relevant, so are reduced cash flows accruing to the French and German operations, and so are increased flows accruing to the South American mine.

Futhermore, international investment is one of the most fertile sources of growth option – see Chapter 13. Such impacts should be allowed for in the appraisal of international investment opportunities.

An overview

International capital budgeting, like its domestic counterpart, focuses upon expected incremental cash flows associated with a project. But international capital budgeting is more complex because of certain factors peculiar to international operations.

There are six main categories of complexity. These embrace situations where exchange controls prevent full remittance of overseas incremental cash generation created via the new project, where part of the parent input is by way of equipment, where exchange rates are not expected to be constant throughout a project's life (and this probably applies to all overseas projects), where different tax rates apply in the host and home country, where royalties and fees are to be paid out of income of the new investment to a group company in the home country and where there are substantial knock-on effects and growth options. These distinctive characteristics are extremely important. They are rarely fully appreciated even within the most sophisticated of companies and the astute treasurer can play a big part in helping his or her company grapple with the difficulties surrounding international investment appraisal. Many poor international investment decisions have been made because of the failure of the multinational company fully to comprehend that it is distributable parent cash flows that matter rather than mere project cash flows.

15

Is the international financing decision different?

Companies – whether they operate within national boundaries alone, or beyond – may borrow in their own domestic capital markets or they may move further afield and tap international markets to finance their operations. The Eurocurrency market is the largest international source of funds and its growth has been astounding. The Eurocurrency market is that market in which banks, often termed Eurobanks, accept deposits and make loans denominated in currencies other than that of the country in which the banks are located. Eurodollars are dollars held in the form of time deposits in banks outside the United States. Euro Deutsche Marks are marks deposited in banks outside Germany. The prefix 'Euro' really means external and refers to funds that are intermediated outside the country of the currency in which the funds are denominated.

The Eurocredit market is defined as the market for loans in currencies which are not native to the country in which the bank officer making the loans is located. The Eurocredit market is concerned with medium- and long-term loans. Multinational companies and governments are the main borrowers.

A Eurobond is an international bond underwritten by an international syndicate and sold in countries other than the country of the currency in which the issue is denominated. This market, too, has seen phenomenal growth over the last two decades.

The Eurobond market

The Eurobond markets possess a number of advantages for borrowers. These include the following:

1. The size and depth of the market are such that it has the capacity to absorb large and frequent issues.

133

2. The Eurobond market has a freedom and flexibility not found in domestic markets. The issuing techniques make it possible to bypass restrictions such as requirements for official authorization, queueing arrangements, formal disclosure, exchange listing obligations and so forth, which govern the issue of securities by domestic as well as foreign borrowers in the individual national markets. All the financial institutions involved in Eurobond issues are subject to at least one national jurisdiction. National authorities can, and sometimes do, make their influence felt, especially when their own currency is used to denominate the issue.

3. The costs of issue of Eurobonds, up to 2½ per cent of the face value of the issue, are relatively low.

4. Interest costs on dollar Eurobonds are competitive with domestic bonds in New York. It is usual that multinationals are able to raise funds at a slightly lower cost in the Eurobond market than in their corresponding domestic market.

5. Maturities in the Eurobond market are suited to long-term funding requirements. Maturities may reach thirty years, but fifteen-year Eurobonds are more common. In the medium-term range, five- to ten-year Eurobonds run into competition with medium-term Eurocurrency loans.

6. A key feature of the Eurobond market is the development of a reliable and extensive institutional framework for underwriting, distribution and placing of securities.

On the other side of the equation, there are a number of special characteristics of the Eurobond market which make it particularly attractive to investors. These include the following features:

1. Eurobonds are issued in such a way that interest can be paid free of income tax or withholding taxes. Besides this, the bonds are issued in bearer form and held outside the country of the investor, enabling the less than scrupulous to evade domestic income tax and maintain anonymity. Some countries' exchange control regulations limit an investor's ability to purchase Eurobonds.

2. Issuers of Eurobonds have, on the whole, an excellent reputation for creditworthiness. Most of the borrowers, whether governments, international organizations or large multinational companies, have first-class reputations. The market is very much orientated to companies with well-known names.

3. A special advantage to borrowers, as well as lenders, is provided by convertible Eurobonds. Holders of convertible are given an option to

exchange their bonds at a fixed price and within a specified period for the stock of the parent company of the financing subsidiary. A bond with a warrant gives the bondholder an option to buy a certain number of ordinary shares at a stated price. The more the price of the underlying share rises, the more valuable the warrant becomes. Since warrants are usually detachable, the bondholder may retain the bond but sell the warrants.

4. The Eurobond market is active both as a primary and as a secondary market. This secondary market expanded in the late 1960s and early 1970s. Eurobonds are traded over the counter both locally and internationally by financial institutions that are ready to buy or sell Eurobonds for their own accounts or on behalf of clients. Just as telephone and telex linkages have integrated foreign exchange markets, so have they integrated the secondary market in Eurobonds. International trading in Eurobonds is greatly facilitated by a clearing house arrangement in Brussels called Euroclear. Participants in Euroclear can complete transactions by means of book entries rather than physical movements of the securities. This has removed the main barrier to secondary market trading, which had been the inability to deliver bonds on time. There are now various other clearing arrangements in the market.

Borrowing internationally

Tapping foreign capital markets may be done by the parent company or a subsidiary borrowing in local markets. There are a number of special advantages associated with such a financial strategy.

Many companies carry on their main operations in countries whose domestic capital markets are comparatively small and possibly subject to drying up. Should the parent company be located in such a country and should that company have fairly substantial needs for cash to invest in order to compete in world markets, then its growth and competitive ability may be constrained by the existence of shallow domestic financial markets, unless it taps international financing sources. This was one of the major problems confronting Novo Industri A/S, the pharmaceutical group based in Denmark, when in 1978 it launched its first dollar convertible Eurobond issue. The economics of the pharmaceutical industry, with its high added value, high research and development levels, high capital intensity and its need for constant innovation, makes access to deep capital markets a necessary precondition to successful competition on a world scale. Novo was aware that the scale of its corporate strategy pivoted about the availability of substantial cash resources on an ongoing basis. It saw its

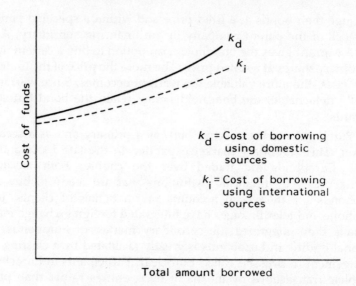

Figure 15.1 The international cost of borrowing.

domestic capital market as being small and subject to periods of illiquidity which meant that, if it wanted to pursue its strategic plan, it was necessary to look outside domestic capital markets.

These kinds of consideration are not too critical for companies based in the UK or the USA, but they can be very relevant in many other countries. Indeed, the lack of depth coupled with the illiquidity of some countries' capital markets may be the historical reasons for most large multinational businesses being based in countries with sophisticated financing sources. This author believes that the lack of ready access to substantial domestic capital markets has constrained the growth of businesses in many smaller European countries and elsewhere in the world.

Besides the benefit of access to deeper financial markets, tapping capital markets outside its home country should enable the international company to take advantage of market imperfections that prevent the Fisher effect from holding in the short term. It will be recalled that, according to the four-way equivalence model developed in Chapter 2, real interest rates (that is, nominal rates adjusted for anticipated inflation) should tend towards equality. But, given that our model is rarely, if ever, totally in equilibrium, the company which has access to world financial markets, rather than just its domestic one, should be able to lower its costs of borrowing. Schematically we would suggest a relationship like that shown in Figure 15.1. It is worth mentioning, however, that when a company taps international financial sources for the first time it generally finds itself paying slightly more than an established borrower in terms of interest rates plus underwriting fees.

The risks of borrowing internationally

International financing can be broadly categorized as falling into three classes embracing the following situations:

1. Financing in the currency in which cash inflows are expected.
2. Financing in a currency other than that in which cash inflows are expected, but with cover in the forward or swap market.
3. Financing in a currency other than that in which cash inflows are expected, but without forward cover or an appropriate swap.

Financing by way of the first two methods avoids foreign exchange risk. With funds raised via the third method, though, foreign exchange risk is taken on. If the international Fisher effect were always to hold as an immutable iron law, and if foreign exchange markets were always in equilibrium, then the benefit accruing to the company through lower nominal interest rates on financing in a hard currency would be offset exactly by the amount by which the harder currency appreciated relative to other currencies. In other words, if the international Fisher effect holds the true cost of funds, at the pre-tax level, would be equal to the nominal interest rates in the home currency and this rate would apply irrespective of whence the international company were to draw its funds. As we know from the earlier discussion, the international Fisher effect does not hold in the short term in the real world, and there is some doubt about whether it holds in the long term. If it is the case that we cannot feel confident about the international Fisher effect asserting itself in the long run, and if it is also the case that exchange rate markets and interest rates are not always in equilibrium, then the international treasurer may seek either to avoid financing risk by one or more of the techniques discussed in Chapters 8–11, or to profit in this area by personal insights. Thus the international treasurer may seek to raise money denominated in overvalued currencies for relatively long maturities; and by the same token will avoid raising funds in undervalued currencies.

Just as disequilibrium in the international Fisher effect can give rise to financing opportunities for the astute corporate treasurer who is prepared to take on foreign exchange risk, so can market imperfections which flow from different tax regimes create opportunities. However, it must be borne in mind that financing in a currency other than that in which cash inflows are expected, but without forward cover, is a risky course of action.

This whole area of foreign currency financing without forward cover is full of pitfalls. Short-cuts are ill-advised. There is no substitute for careful analysis of the interaction between past movements of exchange rates, interest rates and inflation rates.

An overview

International borrowing enables companies to lower their average cost of finance and it may be an important part of the funding equation for companies whose base is within countries with shallow capital markets, as well as for major multinational companies.

International financing can be categorized into three classes. First, a company may borrow internationally in currencies in which it expects cash inflows to accrue. Secondly, it may borrow in a currency other than that in which cash inflows are expected but it may cover foreign exchange exposure. Thirdly, the company may finance itself in a currency other than that in which cash inflows are expected but not take forward cover. The last of these funding options is the most risky. While the interest rate and capital repayments are fixed in foreign currency terms the problem is that, because exchange rates may change, the home currency cost of borrowing is uncertain. It is possible to estimate the true cost of an uncovered foreign borrowing by taking into account expected exchange rate movements and timing of cash flows. This is done using the discounted cash flow technique with cash flows expressed in home currency terms after allowing for expected foreign exchange rate movements. With flows expressed in home currency the calculation of the true cost of the loan (in home currency terms) is the discounted cash flow rate which equates expected inflows and outflows under the financing.

16

The European Monetary System

No overview of foreign exchange markets would be complete without reference, however brief, to the European Monetary System (EMS). Its purpose, structure, functioning, special features, tensions and relative breakdown are summarized in this chapter. It is worth beginning this section by being clear that the EMS is neither a pure fixed exchange rate system nor a pure floating rate mechanism.

The EMS was created in 1979 by the European Union (EU) countries with the dual objectives of establishing a zone of exchange rate stability to encourage trade and growth and of accelerating the convergence and integration of economic policies within the EU.

Principal features of the EMS

The main characteristic of the EMS is the operation of its exchange rate system. The European Currency Unit (ECU) is the nucleus of the EMS. The ECU comprises a basket of fixed amounts of EU currencies.

These fixed amounts are reviewed every five years and can be changed only by official action. The weights of the currencies are calculated by converting their fixed amounts into a common currency (the ECU) at currency market exchange rates. This means that a currency's weight can move in response either to a change in its fixed amount or to a change in its market exchange rate. Official recompositions were intended to correct changes in ECU weights caused by changed economic fundamentals such as underlying inflation rates or due to new entrants into the system.

A currency's ECU value, and so its weight in the ECU, will fluctuate in step with changes in market exchange rates. These market-induced changes in ECU weights will remain small in the absence of a full-scale realignment.

The ECU is used both as the numeraire of the Exchange Rate Mechanism and as a means of settlement between central banks within the EU. Additionally, it exists as a unit of account for official EU business. The ECU is frequently used as a currency of denomination in the international credit and bond markets. Around 3 per cent of international bond issues are denominated in ECUs and some EU countries governments also issue domestic treasury bills in ECUs. However, only around 5 per cent of European trade is invoiced in ECUs. ECU interest rates are equal to a weighted average of the component domestic rates of the EU currencies. In practice, synthetic ECU yields and forward exchange rates are often calculated from a hypothetical basket containing only those currencies with liquid domestic money markets. Note that sterling is a component of the ECU. At the time of writing, however, the British pound was not a member of the exchange rate mechanism (ERM) of the EMS.

The Exchange Rate Mechanism

The central idea underpinning the European Monetary System was to achieve currency stability through coordinated exchange rate management. This would facilitate trade within the EU and set the stage for moves towards a single currency around the end of the twentieth century.

The exchange rate mechanism, a system of flexible exchange rates, was the central plank of the EMS. Countries participating in the ERM would keep the value of their currencies within margins of 2¼ per cent either side of central rates against the other currencies in the mechanism. Sterling, the peseta and the escudo, which joined the ERM several years after its start-up, were allowed to move within margins of 6 per cent upwards and downwards.

The ERM worked by requiring members to intervene in the foreign exchange markets to prevent currencies breaching their ceilings or floors against the other currencies. Thus, if the peseta fell to its floor within the system, the Bank of Spain would be required to buy pesetas and/or sell other ERM currencies to bolster the peseta against its fellow European exchange rates. Other members would be required to help by intervening on behalf of the weak currency. In our example this would prop up the peseta before it fell through its floor.

As a second resort, the country whose currency was under pressure could raise its short-term interest rates to make its currency more attractive to investors. If intervention on the foreign exchanges and adjustment of interest rates failed to stop a currency from moving outside of its ERM limits, a last resort would be a realignment of the central rates to relieve the tensions in the system.

In the early years of the ERM there were several realignments. But from 1987 until the massive tensions of the autumn of 1992, there was none. Many would argue that it was the failure of the mechanism to realign in response to the strength of the Deutsche Mark that led to these very tensions. So let us look at these problems further. But before we do, there are a couple of highly pertinent aspects that require discussion – these relate to European Monetary Union (EMU) and German reunification.

European Monetary Union

Countries may link their currencies together in various ways. At one end of the spectrum would be a relatively light linkage with little sacrifice of independence of monetary policy; at the other, there might be a convergence of policy such that independence is given up altogether. In 1989 a committee headed by Jacques Delors, the then – president of the European Commission, recommended a three-stage transition to a goal of monetary union at the strongly convergent end of the above financial spectrum. The ultimate goal was for European Monetary Union (EMU), a European Union in which national currencies are replaced by a single EU currency managed by a sole central bank operating on behalf of all EU members.

The Delors vision involved three stages. In the first, all EU members would join the ERM. In stage 2, exchange rate margins would be narrowed and certain macroeconomic policy decisions placed under more centralized EU control. In essence, stage 3 of the plan involves the replacement of national currencies by a European currency and the vesting of monetary policy decisions in a European System of Central Banks, similar to the US Federal Reserve System and headed by a European Central Bank.

On 10 December 1991, the leaders of the EU countries met at Maastricht in the province of Limburg at the most southerly tip of the Netherlands. They proposed far-reaching amendments to the Treaty of Rome. These amendments would put the EU squarely on course to EMU. Included in the 250-page Maastricht Treaty were provisions calling for a start to stage 2 of the Delors plan on 1 January 1994 and a start to stage 3 no later than 1 January 1999. In addition to its monetary policy provisions, the Maastricht Treaty proposed steps towards harmonizing social policy within the EU (with rules on workplace safety, consumer protection, and immigration) and towards centralizing foreign and defence policy decisions that EU members currently make on their own.

Despite the optimism of Maastricht, the treaty was soon being viewed with scepticism. Many Europeans began to question whether their countries would be wise to sacrifice control over their national economic policies. The Maastricht Treaty could not come into force until all EU countries had ratified it through national referendum or parliamentary vote. In June 1992 the treaty, in its very first electoral test, was narrowly rejected by Danish voters. Prospects for EMU worsened later that year. In September 1992, ERM parities were hit by speculative attacks that led to the British pound and the Italian lira making their exits from the ERM on 16 September 1992 – coined 'Black Wednesday'. Investors and speculators shifted vast funds out of sterling and the lira into the Deutsche Mark. Both sank well below their ERM floors as the authorities gave up the struggle to keep them within their old bands. On that day, the UK government tried to save the pound by intervening heavily and by announcing an increase in interest rates from 10 per cent to 15 per cent. But this was not enough to stem the flow against sterling and after a steady drain on reserves the British government pulled out and lowered interest rates back to 10 per cent – and all on the same day.

For the next eleven months or so, relative calm returned to the ERM currencies. But, in August 1993 tensions rose again – this time centred on the French franc. France was in a recession with high unemployment yet was unable to cut its very high interest rates much below Germany's because both were within the same currency zone.

One solution might have been for Germany to lower its lending rates, but the Bundesbank, the German central bank, did not contemplate such a move for fear of encouraging inflation at home. The prime duty of the Bundesbank, an independent Central Bank, as set out in its constitution, is to monitor domestic monetary policy. The Bundesbank is required, by law, to put the need for low German inflation before the troubles of the ERM.

Pressure mounted. Finance ministers of EU countries met to find a solution. Their answer was to widen the currency bands for all except the Deutsche Mark and the Dutch guilder to 15 per cent. The mark/guilder band remained at 2¼ per cent. For the rest, the bands were so wide that although the ERM survives in name, at the time of writing, the currencies are effectively floating. With the new bands, a currency could move by 30 per cent – from its ceiling to its floor – against another member without falling out of the system.

One of the key sources of tension for the ERM in its recent years of turmoil flowed from German reunification. Its effects on European currency rates are now considered.

German reunification

The reunification of East and West Germany in 1990 created an economic disturbance that deeply affected the EMS. East German wages, initially far below those in the West, moved upwards as East German workers demanded parity with workers elsewhere in the country. But many East German workers lacked the skills, training and modern equipment of those in the West. Expected flows of private investment to modernize eastern Germany failed to materialize. Coupled with high European recession, the result was high unemployment in the East and a steep fall in East German output. The western side of Germany soon found itself making payments to the East – to support and retrain unemployed workers, to renovate antiquated capital stock, and to clean up the East's polluted environment. By 1991 western Germans were transferring an amount well over 5 per cent of their income to the east. The German government borrowed much of the necessary sums rather than raising taxes. Hence the public fiscal deficit widened sharply.

Further inflationary pressures came from the liberal spending of the East Germans, who had received a liberal trade of their Ostmarks into Deutsche Marks, to purchase the high-quality consumer durables they had been denied under Communism. To halt rising prices, Germany's Bundesbank tightened monetary controls in 1992 and also pushed interest rates to historically high levels. By then the European economies, other than Germany, had been weakening for more than a year. One factor partially underpinning this weakness may have been the German aggregate demand expansion itself, which had already raised interest rates in Germany and throughout the EMS. A second factor behind Europe's recession was continuing slow economic activity in the USA and the resulting real depreciation of the dollar – this moved world demand away from European goods and towards American goods.

Germany's decision to tighten monetary policy passed a problem on to France and Germany's other ERM partners. Should they tighten their own monetary policies in unison with Germany's to maintain ERM exchange rates? Or should they devalue their currencies against the mark as a way of stimulating international demand for their products? While criticizing Germany's tight monetary policy, the ERM partners allowed their own interest rates to rise in line with Germany and thereby resisted devaluation. With EMU seemingly in reach, governments wanted to avoid being forced into a new alignment. The defence of EMS exchange rate levels deepened the European recession outside of Germany. Germany denied any responsibility for the rest of Europe's economic problems and refused to make substantial policy changes, although it could be argued that a temporary withdrawal of the German mark from the ERM might better have kept the ERM on course and avoided the turmoil that subsequently affected exchange rate markets in Europe. The Germans themselves worried that a European central bank, following EMU, would be less zealous than their own Bundesbank in fighting inflation. With unemployment on the rise throughout Europe, job losses were blamed on the European Union's liberal trade and migration policies and the ERM.

Black Wednesday

In June 1992 Denmark, the first country to vote on the Maastricht accord, rejected the treaty by a small margin. Danish rejection raised serious legal problems because amendments to the Treaty of Rome required unanimous approval of all EU members. A similar referendum was scheduled for September in France. The prospect of a French refusal to ratify Maastricht encouraged foreign exchange market participants to gamble that weak currencies would devalue. The first currencies to be hit by speculative attacks were the Finnish markka and the Swedish krona. Neither belonged to the ERM, but both wished for EU membership and had pegged their currencies to the ECU. Finland capitulated on 8 September 1992 letting the markka depreciate steeply against the ECU. Sweden was successful temporarily in defending the krona. Speculation died down only after the Swedish central bank, the Riksbank, allowed interest rates on overnight loans to reach 500 per cent per annum, about 1.35 per cent per day. At the same time, the UK and Italian governments were struggling to keep their currencies above the floors of their ERM bands.

Speculation against the pound and lira continued. By the evening of Friday, 11 September, the Bundesbank had spent $16bn in EMS intervention supporting the lira. The Bundesbank was reluctant to spend any more. Over the weekend the EMS agreed to let Italy devalue its currency by 7 per cent against the ECU. The lira's parity change was the first ERM realignment since January 1987. It signified to players in the foreign exchange market that attacks on other ERM currencies might succeed.

On Tuesday, 15 September, Bundesbank President Helmut Schlesinger was reported in a German newspaper as saying that a broad currency realignment would be needed to ease existing tensions in the ERM. His remark set off a massive speculative attack against the pound and the lira in particular. On 16 September, a day now known as Black Wednesday because of the damage done to the ERM, the pound was allowed to float after the Bank of England lost billions of dollars defending it. This action followed numerous repeated pledges by the British government not to realign. Despite having devalued only two days before, Italy took the lira out of the ERM rather than lose more reserves. Spain devalued the peseta and reimposed exchange controls.

Then the French franc came under attack, despite an inflation rate lower than Germany's. Heavy and prolonged intervention by the Bank of France and the Bundesbank plus a sharp rise in French interest rates eventually extricated the franc from the bottom of its ERM band. After the most turbulent week in ERM history, French voters narrowly approved the Maastricht Treaty on 20 September and thereby gave EMU another chance, albeit a relatively faltering one.

The wake of Black Wednesday

Currency upheavals continued through 1992 and into the spring of 1993. Later in 1992 the Portuguese escudo was devalued, the Spanish peseta devalued again and the Swedish krona and Norwegian krone, although not in the EMS but linked to it, were set afloat. Early in 1993, the Irish punt was devalued, the escudo devalued a second time, and the Spanish peseta devalued a third time. The French franc and Danish krone continued to be under periodic speculative attack. These events took place against deepening recession in the ERM economies, not helped by the Bundesbank's insistence on making only gradual cuts in German interest rates.

In the Spring of 1993, Denmark held a second referendum on the Maastricht Treaty after the EU had given Denmark the right to refuse participation in the common monetary and defence policies which the treaty would create. Second time around, Denmark agreed and the British government followed suit by a narrow parliamentary majority for ratification. By 1993 all EU members but Germany had approved the Maastricht Treaty.

During July of 1993, speculators attacked the French franc and other ERM currencies again after a new disagreement over interest rates between Germany and other ERM members. On Friday 30 July alone, the Bundesbank sold nearly $30bn worth of Deutsche Marks to help prop up the French franc. The Bank of France itself used up all of its foreign reserves in pursuit of this goal. The following Monday, 2 August, ERM rates with the exception of the mark/Dutch guilder rate would float within widened bands of plus or minus 15 per cent around the existing central parities. This change in ERM rules was extended to avoid a formal devaluation of the French franc, a step the French government had pledged to avoid at all costs, while leaving the Bundesbank free to lower German interest rates slowly.

EU leaders insisted that these problems would not alter the Maastricht Treaty's timetable for EMU. Despite such sentiments even the most enthusiastic of European monetary supporters must be sceptical about EMU – at least on timing.

A number of such Euroenthusiasts also believe that more than some of the blame for the turbulence and its mismanagement must be debited to the account of the Bundesbank whose inflexibility was remarkable. The Bundesbank, they claim, might have been more speedy about cutting interest rates; Germany might temporarily have ceded from the ERM in the immediate shadow of reunification with its singular macroeconomic effects, certainly a factor which created divergence from other European economies. Such an argument leads to the conclusion that European prosperity in the early Nineties has been sacrificed on the altar of German reunification, hardly what the ERM was created for.

Cynics might go as far as to say that the whole scenario suited the Bundesbank down to the ground. A widely agreed, smooth ride to EMU would pose the question of the location of a European central bank. If London or Paris were considered strong potential competitors, their claim in the wake of the currency turmoils of 1992 and 1993 must be weakened – presumably in favour of a German location. Conspiracy theories about the monetary turmoil need more evidence than this. But the clues are manifest. And don't forget that moves to a common currency would adversely affect the profits of a number of commercial bankers and the centre of European-time zone banking is London. Hardly surprising that the City of London is less than enthusiastic about EMU.

Where does EMU go from here? With the 1995 entry of Sweden, Finland and Austria into the EU it is very possible to think of a two-speed or three-speed move to a common currency. Germany, Austria and the Netherlands plus one or two others might be in the vanguard of currency integration with the Bundesbank making obvious claims for central bank status within the new system – although Dutch bankers' objections might create real competition.

On 31 May 1995 the European Commission launched a blueprint for achieving a shift to a single currency by the end of the century. Their Green Paper adopts a gradual approach but the Commission remains confident that an unspecified number of countries in the 15-strong European Union will move to a single currency by the beginning of 1999 with the introduction of Euro-banknotes and coins following within a maximum of three years. The Green Paper proposes three stages in transition towards the adoption of the ECU as the new currency of legal tender. These stages are:

1. Phase A. There is a gap of one year between commitment by participating countries and locking of exchange rates.
2. Phase B. The European Central Bank fixes parities and begins operating a single monetary policy.
3. Phase C. The final changeover to the single currency would follow three years later with participating countries' national notes and coins phased out and the ECU becoming their sole legal tender. For participating

countries all cheques, transfers and credit cards would be converted into ECU.

The 74-page Green Paper lists the benefits of a single currency as a more efficient single market, stimulation of trade, growth and employment, elimination of transaction costs and an increase in international monetary stability.

Britain's position outside of the first wave towards a common currency is almost certain. In the longer term, Britain's parliamentary system and culture create problems. Most European countries effectively have coalitions in government with the result that the attempt of the ruling party to engineer an economic boom in the run-up to a general election does not occur – unlike the political environment in Britain. There are many who would argue that Britain's two-party system is well past its sell-by date. When contrasted with its European counterparts, claims that it achieves superior performances are ludicrous. A coalition would avoid all the pointless economically engineered booms before elections and it would mean that economic policies could be aligned with the UK's European neighbours. Of course, this would also mean a complete volte-face in terms of the goals of Britain's political elite, schooled in the pursuit of power accompanied by class conflict. The Us versus Them attitude has failed miserably to achieve success in business or in economic terms for Britain. One of the steps further to dismantle such outdated confrontation is to set a parliamentary example – a British coalition in government. After all, the UK does have rather a good track record of achievement under coalitions.

An overview

The exchange rate mechanism of the EMS, as originally conceived, constrained the fluctuations of participating member countries' currencies relative to one another. Cross rates were defined in terms of units of currency to the ECU and intervention was called for such that there was only modest deviation in exchange rates between ERM currencies, although such currencies would fluctuate substantially against non-ERM countries' exchange rates. The ERM is now operating such wide bands of currency movement for participating countries (mainly plus or minus 15 per cent) as to render its original objectives of a cleavage of exchange rates of ERM members' currencies virtually non-existent. That the German and the Dutch exchange rates remain in a band of plus or minus 2¼ per cent of each other's ECU parities probably puts them in pole position if the race to a common European currency gets firmly under way. The entry of Austria into the EU adds an obvious other state to the front line. Maybe these three countries will move to a common European currency in the twentieth century. The circulation of this currency elsewhere in Europe might well quickly lead to its more widespread adoption. This scenario, or one very like it, is a racing certainty in the early twenty-first century.

17

Why hedge anyway?

In this chapter an attempt is made to summarize the arguments against and in favour of covering corporate exposures to risk. The reader might reasonably raise the point that it is a little bit late in the day to discuss these points – why was such a fundamental issue not raised in Chapter 1?

In defence of the positioning of such a key topic as 'why hedge?' as late as Chapter 17, the author is prepared to advance an argument. But first of all, let it be said that the objection that this chapter could easily have occurred at the very beginning of the book is a valid one. In the end it was felt that because this book is intended as an essentially basic guide to the theory and practice of international financial management, it made more sense to keep the early sections basic. In short, the writer did not wish to put the reader off by raising a series of arguments that, to a large extent, derive from the academic literature on financial management.

Most corporate treasurers take it for granted that hedging is of virtue; it is implicit in their actions. So there is surely a body of theory to justify hedging. But what is it? Such a question is more difficult to answer than you would have thought because a lot of financial theory points in the opposite direction – it favours not hedging at all; so let's look further.

Covering exposures is designed to reduce the volatility of a firm's profits and/or cash generation – see Figure 17.1. Presumably from this, it might be deducted that the idea is to reduce the volatility of the value of the firm. And, presumably, this should lead to enhanced shareholder value. But such a deduction needs to be challenged. While practitioners might accept the virtue of the foregoing argument, almost like motherhood or brown bread, financial academics might not. So what is their argument?

The capital asset pricing model

According to the capital asset pricing model (CAPM), well-diversified international investors should not be willing to pay a premium for

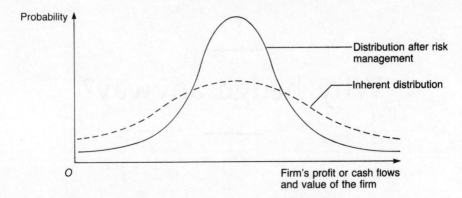

Figure 17.1 The goal of risk management.

corporate hedging activities which they, themselves, can readily replicate by adjusting their own portfolios. Hedging to reduce overall variability of cash flow and profits may be important to managers, compensated according to short-term results, but it is irrelevant to diversified shareholders. The ups and downs of individual investments are compensated by holding a well-diversified portfolio.

CAPM suggests that what matters in share pricing is systematic risk. If exchange risk and interest rate risk are considered to be unsystematic, then their effect can be diversified away by holding a balanced portfolio. On the other hand, if they are systematic and if forward and interest rate instruments are priced according to CAPM, then all that the firm does by entering into hedging contracts is to move along a risk/return trade-off line and this adds nothing to the value of the firm. Indeed, it is arguable that, at the margin, transaction costs in forward contracts may actually destroy value.

We have already introduced one or two CAPM concepts, but since not all readers will be familiar with CAPM perhaps it would be worthwhile to step back and consider its essential ideas. This now follows.

In market equilibrium, a security is expected to earn a return consistent with its unavoidable risk – that is the risk that cannot be avoided by the shareholder via diversification. Unavoidable risk is also termed systematic risk. The greater the unavoidable risk, the greater the return expected by investors in the security. This interaction between anticipated return and unavoidable risk and the valuation of securities is what the capital asset pricing model is all about. The model was developed some thirty years ago and it has been an important part of financial theory ever since. CAPM attempts to explain financial market behaviour. It is relatively simple in basic concept and has wide applicability in the real world.

There are certain key assumptions underpinning the CAPM. First, it is assumed that capital markets are efficient and investors are well informed, transaction costs are zero, there are no restrictions on investment, no taxes and no single investor is large enough to affect the market price of the share. An efficient financial market is one where securities prices reflect all available public information about the economy and about the specific company concerned. The implication is that market prices of individual securities adjust rapidly to new information. As a result, security prices are said to fluctuate randomly about their fundamental values.

The CAPM is concerned with expected returns from an individual share compared with the expected return of the market portfolio. The focus is upon returns in excess of the risk-free rate. The excess return is defined as the expected return less the risk-free return. Thus, for example, for each of the last sixty months, analysts might compute excess returns for the particular share involved and for the market portfolio, as represented by the FT-Actuaries Index. The monthly return for both is given by the end price minus the beginning price plus any dividend paid, all related to the beginning price. From such returns is subtracted the monthly risk-free rate to obtain the excess return.

If we have gone through this process of calculating historic excess returns for a particular share and for the market portfolio, we can plot them. Figure 17.2 shows a possible plot of excess returns for an equity share versus those for the market portfolio. Figure 17.2 indicates that the greater the expected excess return for the market, the greater the expected excess return for the share.

Three key terms are worthy of attention – these are alpha, beta and unsystematic risk; they are referred to in Figure 17.2. Alpha is the intercept of the characteristic line with the vertical axis. If the excess return for the market portfolio were zero, the alpha would be the expected excess return for the share. Theoretically, the alpha for a particular company's share should be zero. If it were less than zero for a particular share, a rational investor should avoid the share because he could do better with some combination of risk-free asset and the market portfolio minus the share concerned. If enough investors avoid it, the price should decline and the expected return will increase. For how long will this go on? Probably until the alpha rises to zero. As the share price declines, its expected return rises and the characteristic line shifts upward until it eventually passes through the origin. Conversely, if the alpha were positive, the opposite adjustment process would occur. Investors would buy the share and this would cause the price to rise and expected return to decline. Hence the assumption that the alpha for any particular share is zero.

Turning next to beta, in the context of Figure 17.2, it may be defined as the slope of the characteristic line. Beta is concerned with the sensitivity of a share's excess return to that of the market portfolio. If the beta of a share is one, it means that excess returns for the share concerned vary

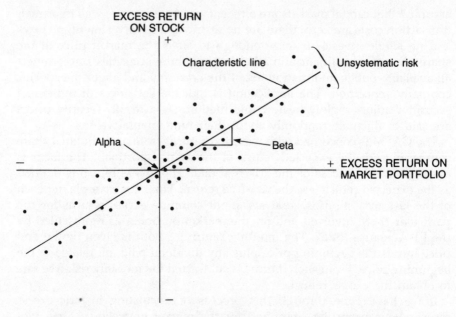

Figure 17.2 Excess return for a share and for the market portfolio.

proportionally with excess returns on the market portfolio. To put it another way, the share has the same unavoidable or systematic risk as the market as a whole. A beta greater than one means that the share's excess return varies more than proportionally with the excess return on the market portfolio. In other words, the share has more systematic risk than the market as a whole. A beta of less than one means that the share concerned has less unavoidable or systematic risk than does the market as a whole.

Also worthy of focus are the terms systematic and unsystematic risk. Unsystematic risk derives from the variability of the share's excess return which is not associated with movements in the excess return of the market as a whole. This risk is described by the dispersion of the estimates involved in plotting a share's characteristic line – see Figure 17.2. In this figure, unsystematic risk is represented by the distance of the dots from the solid line. The higher the dispersion, the greater the unsystematic risk for a share. By diversification of shares held in a portfolio, however, unsystematic risk may be reduced. Consequently the total risk involved in holding an equity share comprises at least two risk components – that is:

Total risk = Systematic risk   + Unsystematic risk
            (non-diversifiable   (diversifiable or avoidable)
            or unavoidable)

Systematic risk is associated with overall market risk – risks that affect firms and securities overall – and, consequently, cannot be diversified away. Even the investor who holds a well-diversified portfolio will be exposed to this kind of risk. The other risk component, unsystematic risk, is unique to a particular company. It is independent of economic, political and other factors that affect shares in a systematic way. Thus, a strike may affect one particular company; a competitor may attack the established position of a company; a technical breakthrough can make a company's existing product obsolete. But, through diversification, this type of risk may be reduced or even eliminated. Thus, not all of the risk involved in holding an equity share is relevant in CAPM terms; some may be diversified away.

Statistical studies suggest that equal holdings of 15 to 20 shares selected randomly are sufficient to eliminate most unsystematic risk from a portfolio. As the number of randomly selected shares held in a portfolio is increased, the total risk of that portfolio is reduced. In this way diversification may reduce the total risk of a portfolio to the point where only systematic risk remains. For the typical leading firm's equity shares unsystematic risk accounts for some 70 per cent of the total risk or variance of the shares; thus systematic risk explains only 30 per cent of the total variability for an individual share price.

CAPM suggests that, assuming capital markets are efficient and investors at the margin are well diversified, the important risk of a share is its unavoidable or systematic risk. As a result, the expected return from a share should be related to its degree of systematic risk – not to its total risk. If we assume that unsystematic risk is diversified away, the expected rate of return for stock j is given by the equation:

$$R_j = R_F + \beta_j(R_M - R_F)$$

where R_F is the risk-free rate, R_M is the expected value of return for the market portfolio, and β_j is the beta coefficient for security j. The greater the beta of a security, the greater the systematic risk and the greater the expected return required. Conversely the lower the beta the lower the systematic risk, and the lower the expected return required.

In equilibrium, the above equation suggests that the relationship between an individual security's expected rate of return and its systematic risk, measured by beta, should be linear. This relationship is known as the security market line. It is illustrated in Figure 17.3. According to CAPM, the risk return trade-off implied by investing in any securities lies along this line. The expected return on a risky security is given by the sum of the risk-free rate plus a premium for risk. This risk premium is needed to induce risk-averse investors to buy a risky security. The expected return for the market portfolio is R_M, consisting of the risk-free rate, R_F, plus the

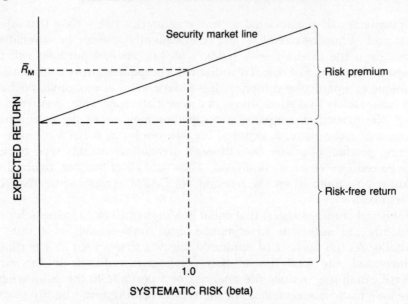

Figure 17.3 The security market line.

risk premium, $(R_M - R_F)$. According to CAPM since the unsystematic risk of a security is eliminated by the well-diversified investor, such investors are not compensated for bearing unsystematic risk.

In the many studies designed to test the CAPM is the real world, results are mixed. Seasonal effects relate to the month and day of the week in which a security trade takes place. Different returns on investment seem to accrue at different times of the week and of the month – which is obviously counter to our theory. The January effect refers to a pattern of excess returns that, on a significant number of occasions, have been observed during that month. And such gains tend to be concentrated in the first few trading days of the month and in the shares of small companies. Excess returns also seem to arise on Fridays. The small firm effect relates to shares of companies with relatively low equity market capitalization – such shares seem to provide higher returns than their larger brethren, all other things being equal.

In short, beta seems to be a major determinant of security returns but by no means all. Certainly there are problems and dangers in blind acceptance and application of CAPM. Although the model should not be expected to produce a perfect measurement of the market equilibration process or of the immutable required return for a particular stock, it does provide us with fairly useful risk/return concepts and a way of approximating the required return for an equity share. The CAPM has its critics – but its applicability to corporate finance is now well established.

What does exposure management aim to achieve?

Certainly, among practitioners at least, the overriding view of the virtue of exposure management is as a device to reduce the variability of the firm's profits, cash flow or valuation caused by changes in interest rates and exchange rates. But there is a countervailing argument advanced by a number of financial academics. Its essence is as follows. Reducing the variability of the firm's returns while leaving their expected level unchanged should have little or no effect on the value of the firm. This view derives from the CAPM. The firm's operations are viewed as a whole. The proposition continues with the idea that well-diversified international investors should not be willing to pay a premium for corporate hedging activities which they can readily duplicate for themselves simply by adjusting their portfolios. Reducing overall variability of profits, cash flow or firm value may be important to managers but it is a matter of irrelevance to diversified shareholders. They even out the ups and downs of individual corporate investments by holding well-diversified portfolios. Rather than being interested in how particular corporations hedge their own outturns, what is important is how the portfolio manager diversifies his or her investments.

The arguments against corporate hedging

Really, the above argument is but one of a battery of attacks drawing their pedigree from the heavyweights of corporate finance. The range arrayed against hedging represents not only the capital asset pricing model but also purchasing power parity.

According to purchasing power parity (PPP), movements in exchange rate offset price level changes. If PPP were to hold immutably and with no time lags there would, so the argument goes, be no such thing as exposure to exchange rate risk and consequently no need to hedge. If the annual rate of inflation in Britain is 10 per cent higher than that in the United States, the pound will depreciate against the US dollar by an appropriate percentage rate. As a result, it follows that there is no relative price risk. If two units of American wheat exchanged for one unit of British beef at the beginning of the year, that same exchange ratio would hold at the end of the year. The mere fact that the pound has depreciated is of no concern. The effect on the American exporter of wheat and the British exporter of beef is of no significance, since the change in nominal prices in their national currencies has been compensated for by the exchange rate change.

But there are numerous problems with this highly simplified version of PPP. Empirical tests have confirmed that the adjustment between changes in price levels and exchange rates is anything but immediate – there are long lags in the PPP relationship working in the real world. Even if, over the long-term horizon, PPP seems to have greater empirical validity there are substantial short-term deviations. If a firm's planning horizon is shorter than that required for PPP to hold then the firm is exposed to exchange risk – and this is probably the case for most firms.

Furthermore, even if PPP holds in the aggregate with respect to the price level indices of two countries it need not – and usually does not – hold for every commodity. In short, the law of one price does not hold. If the increase in the price levels of wheat in the USA and beef in the UK do not correspond to the increases in the inflation levels in their respective countries, there will be a relative price risk. Even if PPP and the law of one price were to hold, prices of a firm's specific inputs and outputs might change relative to each other, and thus expose the firm to risk, which – if caused by unexpected rate changes – must be viewed as exchange rate risk. That there are deviations from PPP and that there are relative price risks for at least some goods imply the presence of exchange risk. The PPP-based argument against hedging is not a substantial one; but the CAPM argument is.

According to CAPM, the essential aspect of risk which matters is systematic risk. If exchange rate risk and interest rate risk are considered to be unsystematic, they can be diversified away by investors in the process of constructing their own portfolios. On the other hand, if currency risk and interest rate risk are systematic and if forward exchange and interest hedge contracts are priced according to CAPM, all that a firm does by entering into these kinds of contract is to move along the security market line. If this is so, then there is no addition to the value of the firm. In the absence of market imperfections, like transaction costs and default risk, the value of a forward contract, at the instant at which it was initiated, should be zero. In reality, there are transaction costs – the bid/offer spread for one. So in the real world, according to this argument, companies could be said to destroy value be entering into forward contracts.

But inevitably there is another point of view. This concerns companies' motivations to avoid financial distress. Greater variability of net cash flow implies a higher probability of bankruptcy. In turn, this affects the firm's cost of funds and its ability to raise finance. In short, despite countervailing CAPM arguments, there is a strong case that avoidance of default risk justifies minimizing variation in cash flows through hedging.

Turning next to arguments against hedging which derive from the Modigliani–Miller (MM) propositions (see 'The cost of capital, corporate finance and the theory of investment', *American Economic Review*, 1958, No. 3), it may be recalled that in relation to corporate gearing they advance the argument that what the firm can do, so can the investor. Extending this argument to the foreign exchange or interest rate domain, the same could be said to apply. Modigliani and Miller's argument suggested that a shareholder could obtain 'home-made leverage' by borrowing on his or her own account. In a similar way, why should the shareholder not obtain 'home-made hedging'? And, like MM's argument that home-made leverage would make corporate gearing irrelevant, so would home-made hedging make corporate hedging irrelevant.

Of course, if for any reason hedging by investors is not as effective as corporate hedging, then it will be in the interest of the shareholders to let the firm manage exchange and interest rate risk. As we have seen in this book heretofore, the main hedging instruments are forward markets, options markets, Eurocurrency markets and foreign money markets. Their nature is wholesale and they deal in minimum amounts that tend to be too large for individual investors. Commercial banks tend to limit access to forward and options markets. True, markets for currency futures exist which are readily accessible to individual investors, so some of the arguments about barriers to entry based on size applying to individual investors disappear. But remember that on financial futures exchanges there is a minimum contract size and the individual investor may be seeking cover at below this level.

Furthermore, there are techniques of currency management which are truly only available at the company, rather than the shareholder, level – for example, leading and lagging of intercompany and third-party payments and judicious transfer pricing of both financial and real resources.

The argument does not stop here. There is an information-based argument too. For the individual investor to hedge, he or she needs to be aware of the level and timing of currency and interest rate exposure for all the companies in the portfolio. Such information is required not only for today but also for future dates. This information may already have been collected by the firm for planning purposes. For the company, information gathering for hedging purposes may involve no additional opportunity cost. In contrast, an individual may have to incur very large costs to obtain similar information – and it is not just for one company either, but for a whole portfolio of investments.

Even though, in an ideal world, shareholders should be able to manufacture home-made hedging it is extremely doubtful whether in the real world this would be either feasible or economic. And this militates in favour of corporate hedging.

But what is the treasurer trying to do by hedging? Surely, even if pursuing a selective hedging policy, the treasurer is not necessarily seeking excess returns, but merely trying to establish a risk/return profile with which the management feels comfortable and is such that it is consistent with the firm's corporate plans. Furthermore, several others with interests in the firm are surely interested in reducing the variance of its returns flowing from currency and interest rate risk exposure. These groups include managers, other employees, financial regulators and creditors.

Employees and managers

Hedging may be argued to be a good thing from the standpoint of employees and managers who, clearly, do not have a diversified portfolio of jobs. Their income stream from employment flows from their single job. By definition investing in their career with one firm implies an undiversified portfolio. Clearly, managers and employees have a strong interest in reducing the variability of profit and cash flows and, in so doing, reducing the risk of financial distress. Another group concerned with reducing the variability of earnings is creditors, who have an obvious interest in their customers reducing their risk of incurring financial distress.

And shareholders too

There is another argument which may be offered against corporate hedging. This concerns the desire of the shareholder for corporate risk. Take a company like BP. Although a British company with a substantial sterling base of shareholders, BP's income flows are essentially in dollars since oil is priced in dollars. If the shareholders' consumption patterns were dollar-based or if shareholders wanted to take on dollar risk it might make sense for BP not to hedge its dollar exposure at all.

Of course, companies are unable to know intimately their shareholders' consumption patterns or desires for risk and this line of reasoning leads to the conclusion that the company might hedge its exposures. The obverse argument contends that if companies were to leave themselves unhedged and communicate the nature of their exposures to shareholders, it would then be up to investors to make their own decisions about whether they wished to take on the company's risk by investing.

In short, the argument is essentially one to the effect that shareholders may actually prefer that a portion of their income stream be denominated – or at least exposed to – foreign currency risk. If the individual shareholder then wished to do so, he would be at liberty to hedge the exposure.

The value of the firm

If risk management is to be logically justified in financial terms, there has to be a positive answer to the question: will exposure management increase the value of the firm? And, furthermore, it is necessary to specify the route by which such value is created.

The equation that is the cornerstone of finance suggests that the value of the firm (V) is a function of expected future net cash flows – $E(NCF)$ – discounted at the firm's cost of capital, k. It can be written as:

$$V = \sum \frac{E(NCF_t)}{(1+k)^t}$$

If the firm's value is to increase, it must do so as a result of either an increase in the expected net cash flows or a decrease in the discount rate.

How might hedging affect the firm's discount rate? If we look at the risks that are usually hedged in an exposure management policy – currency risk, interest rate risk and commodity price risk – we can see that all of these may be interpreted, from the standpoint of modern portfolio theory, as diversifiable risks. Shareholders can manage these risks by holding a diversified portfolio. It follows that active management of these risks should have no effect on the firm's cost of capital. Unless the company is held by undiversified owners, risk management should not increase the expected value of the firm through a reduction in the discount rate.

In the case of a company held by well-diversified investors, exposure management can only be expected to increase the value of the firm through an increase in expected net cash flows. A logical question follows. How can hedging affect the value of the firm's expected net cash flows, as opposed to their variability? It may be argued that avoidance of financial distress creates value via hedging.

Financial distress

In Figure 17.3 it was noted that risk management can reduce the volatility of the cash flows of the firm. Figure 17.4 goes a step further. It indicates that, by reducing cash flow volatility, hedging reduces the probability of the firm getting into financial difficulty and incurring the consequent costs of such distress.

From Figure 17.4 it can be seen that, if V_{FD} is the value of the firm below which financial distress is encountered, hedging may actually reduce the

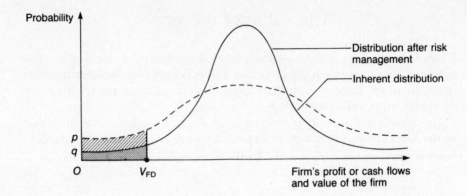

Figure 17.4 Hedging reduces the probability of financial distress.

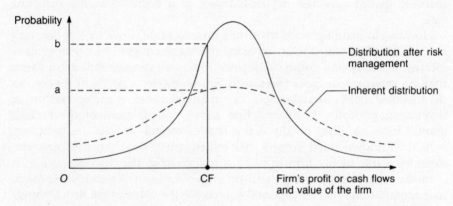

Figure 17.5 Hedging better enables the firm to pursue its desired strategy.

probability of financial distress from point p to point q. Hedging can reduce the potential impact of financial distress by:

1. Reducing the probability of financial distress.
2. Reducing the costs imposed by financial problems.

Clearly, as Figure 17.4 shows, the probability of financial distress may be lowered by hedging.

We can also use the subsequent diagram, Figure 17.5, to point out the virtue of hedging in terms of enabling the firm to achieve its desired corporate strategy, presumably the key to the firm's value. Assume that the cash flow level CF on the horizontal axis of Figure 17.5 is that level of cash generation that the firm needs to undertake to pursue its desired investment plans. Clearly, by hedging, the firm reduces the probability that its cash throw-off will be insufficient to enable it to pursue its planned strategy. As can be seen from Figure 17.5, the probability of its being able to pursue the desired policy from self-generated funds increases greatly from level a to level b as a result of exposure management techniques.

Returning to hedging as a device to lower risk of financial distress, even short of bankruptcy, the possibility of financial distress can impose substantial costs on the firm. These involve higher contracting costs with customers, employees, and suppliers. Companies that provide service agreements or warranties make a long-term commitment to their customers. The value customers place on these agreements and warranties depends on their perception of the financial viability of the firm. If the future of the firm is in doubt, customers will place less value on the service back-up and warranties and may turn to a competitor or demand a lower price to compensate. Either way, there is an evident impact upon profit and cash generation of the firm.

The essential argument may be summarized as follows. The marketing of a firm's product may be eased by a stable corporate track record since buyers want some assurance that the firm will stay in business to service and product and to supply parts. By a similar line of argument, potential employees may be scared off by a volatile earnings record which could suggest less job security. To compensate for this, employees may demand higher salaries and perks.

With the probability of financial distress increased by an absence of hedging, suppliers of debt capital might demand higher returns to compensate for higher expected bankruptcy costs and/or they might negotiate tighter debt covenants. Either way, the tendency would be for the cost of debt to increase. In parallel, it could be argued that, *ceteris paribus*, a reduction in the probability of financial distress or default would lower the cost of debt and increase the firm's debt capacity.

The reader might believe that a more realistic model of corporate valuation conforms to that following:

$$V_F = \Sigma \, V_i - P(\sigma)$$

where V_F is the value of the firm, V_i is the net present value of each of the firm's parts and $P(\sigma)$ is a penalty factor that reflects the impact on after-tax cash flows of the total risk of the firm. Note that this formula, which has some guru support, is not consistent with CAPM ideas – the penalty factor is a function of total risk, not just systematic risk. And, if you think about it, firms usually go broke because of total risk rather than systematic risk. Anyway, the above proposition of corporate value would obviously suggest that hedging is a good thing for shareholders because, in lowering the penalty factor, corporate value is enhanced.

An overview

Why hedge anyway? Well, essentially because corporate hedging lowers the probability of financial distress for the company concerned. This is good news for managers and employees who do not hold a diversified portfolio of jobs. It is good news for customers who are relying on their suppliers remaining in business to provide after-sales service and so on. From the standpoint of the provider of debt finance, a lower probability of financial distress will result in a lower cost of debt and, perhaps, a higher debt capacity for the hedged company.

Furthermore, a firm may wish to increase the level of cash generation to some extent in order to increase the probability of its having sufficient investment funds available to pursue its desired corporate strategy – and, after all, it is this desired strategy which is the driver of cash generation and hence shareholder value.

The above line of reasoning points towards the virtue of hedging despite arguments against which draw upon the capital asset pricing model, purchasing power parity and the Modigliani–Miller hypothesis.

18

Economic exposure revisited

Economic exposure is concerned with the present value of future operating cash flows to be generated by a company's activities and how this present value, expressed in parent currency terms, changes following exchange rate movements. Ideas about hedging economic exposure, complicated as they are, are based upon this definition.

Nowadays another view of economic exposure is emerging and it is one which may be more useful and powerful from the standpoint of providing information upon which the risk-averse firm may plan a hedging strategy. The term 'macroeconomic exposure' has been coined for it and it goes far beyond mere exposure to exchange rate changes. Macroeconomic exposure is the focus of this short chapter. Work on this topic is in its infancy. However, the author is of the opinion that the potential for using macroeconomic exposure techniques is not to be under-rated. Perhaps in ten or twenty years' time, it will be this kind of exposure that is the main focus of the corporate treasurer's job. So what is macroeconomic exposure?

Macroeconomic exposure

Macroeconomic exposure is concerned with how a firm's cash flows, profit and hence value change as a result of developments in the economic environment as a whole. This necessarily includes movements in exchange rates, interest rates, inflation rates, wage levels, commodity price levels and other shocks to the system. All firms are clearly vulnerable to this kind of exposure. The economic shock may emanate from the home economy or abroad. The idea behind managing macroeconomic exposure is first of all to identify the nature of the exposure and then to manage it by hedging techniques.

The identification of a firm's sensitivity to macroeconomic variables may be established by determining the way in which cash flow, profits and value vary in response to changes in key economic variables, such as interest rates, price levels, exchange rates, commodity prices and so on. The relevant variables are first of all put forward as a result of deductive reasoning. They are then fed into a statistical model, with recent values set against them with the objective of establishing the coefficients of sensitivity using regression analysis techniques. Data must be available for a sufficiently long period of time and it is usual to begin this analysis by breaking down data by product, strategic business unit, country of operations and so on although analysis may, equally well, be done on a total firm basis.

The analysis

Let us assume that an analysis has been undertaken for a UK-based company in terms of estimating, by regression techniques, the percentage rate of change in the firm's real cash flows in response to unanticipated changes in price levels abroad and at home, the exchange rate, domestic and foreign interest rates and relative prices of significant inputs. Let us assume that this analysis produces the results, in terms of the exposure coefficients, noted in Table 18.1.

The figures in the second column of the table indicate, for example, that a 1 per cent unanticipated increase in UK price levels will lead to a fall

Table 18.1 Effect of a 1 per cent unanticipated change in macroeconomic variables on the firm's real cash flows

Variable	Exposure coefficient	Real effect (£m)	Example of 1% change
Domestic price level	−0.6	−0.45	Retail prices move from 100 to 101
Foreign price level	0	0	
Exchange rate	−0.5	−0.375	$/£ rate moves from 1.80 to 1.7820
Domestic interest rate	−0.8	−0.6	Interest rates move from 10% to 10.1%
Foreign interest rate	0.2	+0.15	US interest rates move from 10% to 10.1%
Commodity prices	−0.2	−0.15	Copper prices move from £1,500 per tonne to £1,515 per tonne
Relative prices	0.6	+0.45	Output price index relative to RPI increases from 1 to 1.01

of 0.6 per cent in real cash flows. The table shows that real UK cash flows are insensitive to changes in foreign price levels. But the table goes on to indicate that, for a 1 per cent unanticipated rise in the exchange rate, cash flows drop by 0.5 per cent holding other variables constant. As the table shows, the sensitivity in this case is to the sterling–dollar exchange rate. Depending upon the reality of macroeconomic relationships for the firm concerned, it might be the case that the critical exchange rate to be included in the analysis turned out to be sterling–yen movements or sterling–Deutsche Mark fluctuations. The next exposure coefficient which is highlighted is the domestic interest rate. Here, the indication is that for a 1 per cent unanticipated rise in interest rates, real cash flow falls by 0.8 per cent. The effect which the domestic interest rate has upon cash flow may ripple through other lead indicators. For example, one of the key lead indicators in the building materials industry is housing starts but this may be predicated, in turn, upon interest rate levels.

The next exposure coefficient shown in the table, foreign interest rates, indicates that for a 1 per cent unanticipated change in their level, real cash flow of the firm rises by 0.2 per cent. Again, it may be the case that only the German or US interest rate is of any relevance since it may impinge upon competitors located in these respective countries.

The table goes on to indicate that a 1 per cent unanticipated rise in commodity prices results in a 0.2 per cent fall in real cash flow of the firm. Clearly what constitutes relevant commodity prices will vary from industry to industry. Cement prices may be critical for one industry but not for another. Steel prices may be significant in one business and not another. And it may be the case that one would wish to allow for more than one critical commodity for a particular business unit. Finally, there is reference in the table to relative prices. This measures the firm's output and/or input prices relative to the general price level. A 1 per cent increase in this ratio results in an increase of 0.6 per cent in the firm's real cash flows.

If the firm's expected real cash flows in the base case are £75m, then by multiplying the exposure coefficient by this amount, we obtain the real effect of changes in the macroeconomic variable detailed in the third column of Table 18.1. We have assumed that the exposure coefficients are partial. This means that they refer to the sensitivity of real cash flows to changes in each variable while other variables are held constant. Thus the domestic interest rate coefficient indicates the effect of a change in domestic interest rates with all other variables held constant.

Hedging

Once sensitivity measures have been established, financial instruments may be used to hedge exposures. For example, assume that the firm for whom data are given in Table 18.1 were only concerned with hedging its dollar/sterling currency exposure, the firm would deal in the forward market for such an amount that should there be a 1 per cent strengthening in the dollar against sterling, then the firm would make a profit of £375,000. This would offset the lost £375,000 shown in the table.

On the basis of the exchange rate data set out in Table 18.1, the firm would buy twelve-month forward dollars of approximately $67m. Buying this amount of dollars for delivery in twelve months implies that, should there be a depreciation of sterling equivalent to 1 per cent against the dollar, the firm obtains a cash gain of £375,000 which offsets the cash flow loss resulting for the trading depreciation of sterling. Through this means, then, the firm might hedge itself against changes in the sterling/dollar exchange rate.

Other financial contracts, such as interest rate futures, may be used to hedge interest rate exposures. The same can be done in respect of commodity futures. So if the firm wished to hedge exchange rate, interest rate and commodity exposure, it would use foreign exchange forwards, interest rate futures and commodity futures. However, some extra care has to be taken. This arises because of the fact that the value of the forward contract is sensitive to interest rate changes and the value of the interest rate and commodity futures depends upon the exchange rate. The effect of this is that the size of each hedge contract depends upon the size of other hedge contracts.

And, of course, tax is a major impediment to efficient hedging using macroeconomic exposure techniques – as it is currently with the hedging of economic exposures.

Interest rates invariably key

In connection with the effect upon corporate cash flow of interest rate and exchange rate changes, the evidence is that the effects of changes in world interest rate levels have been greater and more statistically pronounced than the effects of exchange rate changes. This would suggest that the traditional method of looking at economic exposure – that is by focusing upon foreign exchange rate changes – is likely to achieve less good results than the methodology which focuses upon macroeconomic exposure.

Some experts suggest that, in making an appraisal using macroeconomic exposure, the analyst should disaggregate cash flows in terms of products, subsidiaries and types of cash flow. Such an analysis would produce a better understanding of the operations of the total corporate entity but it is not necessarily clear why such a breakdown would give us better information with which to undertake a hedging policy. After all, if we are concerned with undertaking a covered strategy designed to eliminate macroeconomic exposure at the group level, it would seem that it is group exposures that are critical rather than exposures at the level of the individual operating companies. Admittedly, if the group were to have a large number of subsidiary or associate companies, which might not be wholly owned, then there could be some value in undertaking hedges at the levels of the individual companies. However, if this is not so then there would seem to be no great advantage beyond that of greater informational content and understanding, to be obtained from carrying out the analysis to the disaggregated level.

Experiments with macroeconomic exposure

It is easy to argue that future developments in corporate hedging policy will take place in the macroeconomic exposure arena. Clearly, assuming that the statistical analysis is undertaken correctly, then macroeconomic exposure analysis provides a tool which gets to the very heart of cash flow and profit uncertainty. At the present point in time, there are a number of companies experimenting with the application of this technique. We predict that within the next two decades the major emphasis of exposure management will be in this direction.

An overview

Macroeconomic exposure is concerned with how the firm's profits, cash flow and value change as a result of developments in the economic environment as a whole – that is, within the total framework of exchange rates, interest rates, inflation rates, wage levels, key commodity prices and other shocks to the system.

The sensitivity of a firm's profits, cash flow and/or value to changed macroeconomic variables may be established using regression analysis techniques. The resulting coefficients can provide the wherewithal for the firm to undertake a hedging strategy.

The study of macroeconomic exposure analysis and its implied hedging possibilities is in its infancy, but it promises to be one of the most powerful tools available in exposure management. At the moment, this technique is at the leading edge of treasury management. Within the next couple of decades its application will probably become commonplace.

Questions and answers

To develop understanding of the concepts and figuring presented in this book, readers are invited to put their acquired expertise to the test by attempting a few questions – some quantitative, some qualitative. There is first a series of numerical foreign exchange rate questions which is followed by a case study. Answers appear at the end of this chapter.

Numerical questions

Consider the tabulation below which comprises foreign exchange quotations given by a bank to a customer. The figures given are for the foreign currency against sterling and the word 'premium' or 'discount' implies that the foreign currency quoted at the head of the column is at the premium or discount, respectively.

	$	DM
Spot	1.6915–25	2.20–2.20¼
	Premium	Premium
1 month forward	1–0.90 cents	2½–2¼ pfennigs
2 months forward	1.60–1.50 cents	4½–4¼ pfennigs
3 months forward	2.10–2.00 cents	5½–5¼ pfennigs

1. At what rate will the bank buy spot dollars against sterling?
2. At what rate will the customer sell dollars one month forward against sterling?
3. At what rate will the customer buy Deutsche Marks spot against sterling?

4. At what rate will the customer buy dollars two months forward against sterling?

5. At what rate will the bank sell dollars two months forward against sterling?

6. At what rate will the bank buy Deutsche Marks three months forward against sterling?

7. At what rate will the bank buy dollars three months forward against sterling?

8. At what rate will the customer sell dollars three months forward against sterling?

9. At what rate will the bank buy Deutsche Marks one month forward against sterling?

10. At what rate will the customer sell Deutsche Marks on a two-month forward option against sterling?

11. At what rate will the customer sell Deutsche Marks on a three-month forward option against sterling?

12. At what rate will the customer buy dollars on a two-month forward option against sterling?

13. At what rate will the bank sell Deutsche Marks three months forward, option over three months against sterling?

14. At what rate will the customer sell Deutsche Marks two months forward, option over the second month, against sterling?

15. At what rate will the customer sell Deutsche Marks three months forward, option over the second and third months, against sterling?

16. At what rate will the customer buy dollars two months forward, option over the second month, against sterling?

For questions 17–20 calculate the annual forward premium/discount, state which currency is at the premium, and indicate where interest rates should be higher if interest rate parity is holding.

17. Sterling versus dollars one month. Assume that you are a buyer of dollars.

18. Sterling versus dollars three months. Assume that you are a buyer of sterling.

19. Sterling versus dollars three months. Assume that you are a seller of dollars.

20. Sterling versus Deutsche Marks two months. Assume that you are a buyer of sterling.

Bramit Investment Trust plc

Bramit is a UK-based, and sterling-denominated, investment trust specializing principally in taking stakes in unquoted investments in the UK and the USA. Bramit's assets of £400m are currently split into around £200m of non-listed investments (not quoted on a stock exchange) and some £200m of quoted investments. A large part of the portfolio of assets quoted on stock exchanges is made up of previously non-listed investments that have prospered and eventually obtained a stock market quote. Within this total is included some US$300m of investments in American companies. The exchange rate at the time of this analysis is $1.70 = £1.

The trust has a team of six investment managers concentrating upon new, unquoted investment opportunities and two looking at the quoted sector. The management team is based in the UK but frequent trips to the USA are necessitated. Investments in already quoted investments are generally the result of perceived stock market anomalies rather than strategic views about a particular sector or industry.

Primarily venture capitalists looking at a company's abilities to generate cash, the majority of Bramit's investments result from management buy-ins or buy-outs from existing groups. The decision to invest generally depends upon a company's potential to return Bramit's investment and required return within a five-year period. Every six months, Bramit's portfolio is revalued for reporting purposes and this is incorporated into balance sheet value. Quoted investments are valued according to stock market prices but non-quoted investments lack this objectivity for valuation purposes. In each balance sheet they are valued by directors and confirmed by the auditors using very conservative valuation techniques based on the present value of estimated future cash flows discounted at relatively high rates. Bramit receives dividend income from its US and British investments and this currently offsets, almost exactly, salaries, expenses and interest costs. Dividends received from US investments approximate US$3m. Dividends paid to Bramit's shareholders come from realized gains on selling investments.

One of the larger UK investment trusts, Bramit has a market capitalization of approximately £370m and trades, in common with other trusts, at a discount to its asset value. The proximity of the share price to the asset value is a reflection of the market's estimation of the trust, and as Bramit trades fairly closely to its asset value it appears that the market thinks well of the company. One criticism often made of Bramit is that its gearing, at 5 per cent, is low and should be nearer the sector norm for investment trusts of 35 per cent, measured in terms of debt to the aggregate of equity and borrowings. Its existing borrowings are 100 per cent sterling loans.

The board has recently formally acknowledged these comments and is considering increasing borrowing levels.

A further concern of the board is the effect of exchange rate movements upon the asset value of Bramit. As investors in an investment trust are interested primarily in the asset value of the fund, the board is uncomfortable about the effect of exchange rate movements upon that value.

Bramit has a number of opportunities which it wishes to take advantage of; these are split between investments in the UK, Holland, France, Germany and Spain. In order to take advantage of these opportunities as they arise, Bramit is establishing a separate fund called the Eurobram Fund. Of its £200m capital, half is to be subscribed by Bramit with the balance to come from a small number of institutions. It is anticipated that the fund will be fully invested within one year and that the geographic division of its investments will be 75 per cent UK and 25 per cent continental European. The decision to invest in Europe, aside from the UK, like the decision to have a proportion of Bramit's funds invested in the USA, is strategic and decisions on individual investments in these countries will depend, according to the Bramit financial director, Laurie Coleman, upon prospective local currency cash flows back to Eurobram within a five-year time horizon.

The problem

It is precisely this last point that creates a problem for the trust. The investor market makes decisions on investment trusts based upon sterling values. But Bramit has made part of its investments on the basis of US dollar cash flows. At present the company undertakes no foreign exchange hedging. Hence, to the extent that the US dollar/sterling exchange rate changes, Bramit carries a currency exposure which is crystallized every six months on the published balance sheet as a movement to, or from, shareholders' funds.

While Bramit management would wish to be judged upon its ability as an astute investment management team the firm is, according to Laurie Coleman, 'being assessed, in part, on our ability as currency speculators'. This would be reasonable if the assessment were made with the same five-year time horizon as that adopted by Bramit in terms of its investment decisions coming to maturity. It would then be a valid comment upon Bramit's strategic decision to invest in the UK and the USA. Unfortunately, semi-annual reporting requirements mean that commentators focus upon the movement in shareholders' funds each six months and react accordingly. It has been argued, in a recent board meeting, that Bramit would benefit if all movements to shareholders' funds caused by exchange rate fluctuations could be eliminated. If this could be achieved then any change in the value of the trust would be directly attributable to the skills and expertise of the management as investment managers and not distorted by uncontrollable movements in the exchange rate.

Discussion questions

1. In worrying about changed values, is the board of Bramit focusing upon a transaction, translation or economic exposure? Why? Consequently, is the board right to be concerned about the effect of the exchange rate movements? Why?
2. What is the rationale of trying to minimize or eliminate Bramit's foreign exchange exposure?
3. Given the problem, what possible solutions would you propose? Weigh up the relative merits of such solutions.

Answers to numerical questions

It is best to answer any problem about forward rates by first specifying the outright forward quotations. Remember that the bid/offer spread on the quote for the forward rate is always wider than that on the spot quote. From this it follows that the premia stated must be deducted from the spot figures. This gives outright forward quotations as below:

	£/$	£/DM
Spot	1.6915–1.6925	2.20–2.20¼
1 month forward	1.6815–1.6835	2.17½–2.18
2 months forward	1.6755–1.6775	2.15½–2.16
3 months forward	1.6705–1.6725	2.14½–2.15

The answers to the questions now follow relatively easily. Remember that if the customer is buying a foreign currency (i.e. the bank is selling the foreign currency) one should look to the left-hand column; if the customer is selling the foreign currency (i.e. the bank is buying the foreign currency), one should look to the right-hand column.

1. Bank buys dollars = Customer sells dollars =
   Right-hand column = 1.6925.
2. Customer sells dollars = Bank buys dollars =
   Right-hand column = 1.6835.
3. Customer buys Deutsche Marks = Bank sells Deutsche Marks =
   Left-hand column = 2.20.

4. Customer buys dollars = Bank sells dollars =
   Left-hand column = 1.6755.

5. Bank sells dollars = Customer buys dollars =
   Left-hand column = 1.6755

Questions 4 and 5 have the same answer, of course.

6. Bank buys Deutsche Marks = Customer sells Deutsche Marks =
   Right-hand column = 2.15.

7. Bank buys dollars = Customer sells dollars =
   Right-hand column = 1.6725.

8. Customer sells dollars = Bank buys dollars =
   Right-hand column = 1.6725.

Again questions 7 and 8 have the same answer.

9. Bank buys Deutsche Marks = Customer sells Deutsche Marks =
   Right-hand column = 2.18.

For the next few questions we are looking at forward options. Remember that this is not a currency option but a forward contract under which the customer has the right to deliver within a particular period of time. The bank quotes the worst rate in the period over which the customer has the option to deliver.

10. Customer sells Deutsche Marks = Bank buys Deutsche Marks =
    Right-hand column. Option over period from spot to month 2 inclusive. Worst rate = 2.20¼.

11. Customer sells Deutsche Marks = Bank buys Deutsche Marks =
    Right-hand column. Option over period from spot to month 3 inclusive. Worst rate = 2.20¼.

12. Customer buy dollars = Bank sells dollars =
    Left-hand column. Option over period from spot to month 2 inclusive. Worst rate = 1.6755.

13. Bank sells Deutsche Marks = Customer buys Deutsche Marks =
    Left-hand column. Option over period from spot to month 3 inclusive. Worst rate = 2.14½.

14. Customer sells Deutsche Marks = Bank buys Deutsche Marks =
    Right-hand column. Option over period from month 1 to month 2 inclusive (this is the second month). Worst rate = 2.18.

15. Customer sells Deutsche Marks = Bank buys Deutsche Marks =
    Right-hand column. Option over period from month 1 to month

3 inclusive (this gives the second and third months). Worst rate = 2.18.

16. Customer buys dollars = Bank sells dollars =
Left-hand column. Option over period from month 1 to month 2 inclusive (this is the second month). Worst rate = 1.6755.

Questions 17–20 inclusive look at forward premium/discount.

17. You are a buyer of dollars = Bank sells dollars = Left-hand column.

$$\text{Forward premium/discount} = \frac{1.6815 - 1.6915}{1.6915} \times \frac{12}{1} \times 100\%$$

$$= 7.09\% \text{ p.a.}$$

Dollar at premium.
Eurosterling one month interest rates higher than Eurodollar one-month interest rates.

18. You are a buyer of sterling = You are a seller of dollars = Bank buys dollars = Right-hand column.

$$\text{Forward premium/discount} = \frac{1.6725 - 1.6925}{1.6925} \times \frac{12}{3} \times 100\%$$

$$= 4.73\% \text{ p.a.}$$

Dollar at premium.
Eurosterling three-month interest rates higher than Eurodollar three-month interest rates.

19. You are a seller of dollars = Bank buys dollars = Right-hand column.

$$\text{Forward premium/discount} = \frac{1.6725 \times 1.6925}{1.6925} \times \frac{12}{3} \times 100\%$$

$$= 4.73\% \text{ p.a.}$$

Dollar at premium.
Eurosterling three-month interest rates higher than Eurodollar three-month interest rates.

20. You are a buyer of sterling = You are a seller of Deutsche Marks = Bank buys Deutsche Marks = Right-hand column.

$$\text{Forward premium/discount} = \frac{2.16 \times 2.20\frac{1}{4}}{2.20\frac{1}{4}} \times \frac{12}{2} \times 100\%$$

$$= 11.59\% \text{ p.a.}$$

Deutsche Mark at premium.
Eurosterling two-month interest rates higher than Euro Deutsche Mark two-month interest rates.

Suggested answers to the Bramit Investment Trust questions

Question 1

Bramit has two kinds of exposure. To take the simpler first, the company receives US dollar dividends from its US investments. This clearly creates a transaction exposure. The more complicated exposure concerns the fluctuation sterling value of US dollar investments. At first sight this looks like a pure translation exposure, but we need to look more closely. Remember that Bramit revalues its portfolio of US dollar investments every six months and that, for quoted companies, the revaluation is based on stock market values and, for unquoted companies, Bramit calculates the present value of future cash flows. Both values represent economic values. The foreign exchange exposure that Bramit carries is basically to changes in the sterling/dollar exchange rate as applied to a dollar economic value. As such we are looking at an economic exposure. Admittedly we can also categorize this item as a translation exposure. It is, in fact, both an economic and translation exposure.

Thus the board seems right to be worrying about these exposures – they are respectively transaction exposures on dividends and, on the value of the US dollar portfolio there is a translation exposure and an economic exposure. We have argued earlier in this book that management should be concerned with managing transaction and economic exposures.

Question 2

In trying to eliminate exposure the board is trying to smooth out fluctuations in the value of the dollar portfolio, when converted to sterling, based on changed exchange rates. In being concerned with this, there is an assumption that investors have invested in Bramit for its ability to manage its portfolio rather than being concerned with the dollar nature of its US portfolio. Perhaps this is true. But some might argue that investors have put their money into Bramit because they want to back the company's investment abilities at the same time as taking on a dollar speculation. This argument does not hold up too well. Shareholders interested in this kind of speculation could presumably achieve it, should they wish to do so, via a speculation to buy dollars. Why should they buy into Bramit to do a speculation which can more readily be achieved via the futures or options markets? The decision to minimize exposures is therefore based on the presumption that investors are interested in sterling value *per se*; in other words they are not interested in dollar speculation.

Question 3

Bramit has two problems: one is concerned with US dollar dividend exposures and the other with economic values of investments. The solution to the first problem is relatively easy: Bramit could sell the expected dollar dividends forward to eliminate foreign exchange rate changes.

The major problem, though, is one of economic exposure. Set out below are various routes by which the exposure could be eliminated. These include use of:

1. Financing techniques.
2. Swaps.
3. Forwards.
4. Futures.
5. Currency options.

First we look at financing. Bramit's balance sheet, on the basis of the data in the case, would look something like that set out below:

	£m		£m
Dollar investments	176	Shareholders' funds	380
Sterling investments	224	Sterling debt	20
	400		400

Following the raising and investment of finance for the new Eurobram fund, Bramit's investments are likely to show the following currency denomination:

	Sterling values £m
Dollar investments	176
Sterling investments	224 + 150
Continental European investments	50
	600

If the European investments are mainly in EMS currency countries, then ECU financing would provide a logical hedge. If we wished to raise appropriate finance to hedge the currency of assets we should look for £200m of new debt. This might be raised in ECU to the equivalent of £50m and in US dollars to the equivalent of £150m. The rationale for raising this next tranche of debt substantially in US dollars is to hedge the existing dollar assets in Bramit's portfolio. After this, the Bramit group balance sheet would look as follows:

	£m		£m
Dollar investments	176	Shareholders' funds	380
Sterling investments	374	Sterling debt	20
Continental European investments	50	ECU debt	50
		Dollar debt	150
	600		600

The currency of liabilities is now not far out against the currency of assets. If Bramit wished, it could achieve almost complete elimination of exposure by swapping £20m of sterling debt into dollar debt. Bramit's debt to capital employed ratio can be seen to be 37 per cent, marginally above the sector norm. Incidentally, if this route is followed Bramit would not sell US dollar-denominated dividends forward for sterling, but would use the dividends to pay dollar interest. Indeed Bramit may have to buy dollars forward to pay for and eliminate exposure on interest payments net of dividend receipts.

Using swaps is a variant on the above. To finance the Eurobram investment Bramit might raise £200m in sterling. Its balance sheet immediately following this and assuming investment in the Anglo-European portfolio would appear as follows:

	£m		£m
Dollar investments	176	Shareholders' funds	380
Sterling investments	374	Sterling debt	220
Continental European investments	50		
	600		600

Bramit now swaps £50m of sterling debt for ECU debt and also swaps £170m of sterling debt into dollar debt, the objective being to balance currency denomination of assets and liabilities. The balance sheet then appears as below.

	£m		£m
Dollar investments	176	Shareholders' funds	380
Sterling investments	374	Sterling debt	–
Continental European investments	50	ECU debt	50
		Dollar debt	170
	600		600

The currency configuration of liabilities is now virtually as for the currency of assets. The point made about dollar dividends not being sold forward applies here equally well as to the discussion on financing techniques mentioned above.

Using forwards involves a different technique. Let us first look at the value of the dollar portfolio. This currently stands at $300m, that is £176m at current exchange rates. To achieve the required hedge Bramit must start by forecasting the value of its dollar portfolio at the end of the hedge period – say six months ahead; this is the assumed next reporting date. If Bramit estimates that the value of the dollar portfolio by then will be $400m, then it sells $400m forward for six months against sterling. The cost of forward cover will be $1.70 plus or minus interest differentials. Let us assume, to keep things easy, that there is no interest differential – hence the forward rate would be $1.70. If the exchange rate at the period end is $1.70, Bramit's dollar portfolio would be worth £235m. But if the exchange rate changes to $2.00, the value of the portfolio would be £200m – a drop of £35m due to exchange rate movements. Remember, though, that Bramit has entered into a forward contract to sell US$400m at $1.70. At the end of the period, the foreign exchange rate is £2.00. So, to obtain dollars to deliver against the forward contract Bramit buys these in at $2.00 in the spot foreign exchange market. This will cost £200m. It has a forward contract to sell US$400m at $1.70, that is £235m. The company makes a cool £35m profit to counter the drop in the value of the dollar portfolio. It should be mentioned that, using this technique, if the dollar strengthened then Bramit would make a loss on the closing out of the forward contract which would be deducted from the gain in portfolio value to give, again, a net value of £235m. In order to maintain cover in the future, Bramit should enter into a further forward contract to sell US dollars for the next six months based on the estimated dollar portfolio value six months on at the appropriate forward rate.

Bramit could equally well use futures contracts under which it contracts to sell dollars for the appropriate period in the financial futures market. The operation of such cover is essentially as per the forward mechanism except that margin requirements must be met. Furthermore, Bramit could use the forward or futures technique to cover the ECU exposure on its continental European portfolio in the Eurobram Fund.

Lastly, Bramit could use currency options to cover its exposure. Again, we use the dollar exposure as an example. Bramit begins by estimating the value of its dollar portfolio at the end of the next reporting period, say six months away. Again, assume that this is $400m. At an exchange rate of $1.70, the sterling value would be £235m. But if the foreign exchange rate were to move to $2.00, then the sterling value falls to £200m. To counter this potential loss, Bramit would buy a six-month option to sell $400m at, say, the present exchange rate of $1.70. If the exchange rate remains at $1.70, Bramit will clearly not exercise the option: it will let it lapse. But if the exchange rate moves to $2.00, Bramit exercises the option at $1.70 and thereby makes a profit of $35m. Clearly, through this mechanism the effect of changed exchange rates is eliminated. The beauty of the currency option mode of cover can be seen when the dollar strengthens. If the exchange rate at the next reporting date is $1.50 rather than $2.00, the dollar portfolio is worth, in sterling terms, £266m – and Bramit will logically let the currency option lapse (or sell it on in secondary market for time value, if any). With the currency option mode of cover, Bramit can be seen to get the best of both worlds – which is what the currency option premium is paid for. Again, a rolling cover is called for based on estimates of the dollar portfolio six months away.

But there is a problem that we have avoided so far. Cover via forward, futures and currency options may create taxable gains and this might favour the use of the first two techniques, namely financing and swaps. The exact tax treatment is too complicated for this text; suffice to say that a definite problem exists.

Further reading

The problems created by changing foreign exchange rates are extraordinarily complex. This book has set out to provide the essentials of this difficult topic. The hope of the author is that readers have now had their appetites whetted for more. With this in mind, a brief reading-list of books is provided here. All of the books are considered ideal for the next step in the interested reader's studies, and thus exclude very mathematical or very advanced texts – despite there being some excellent works in both these areas.

Abdullah, F. A. (1987) *Financial Management for the Multinational Firm*, Englewood Cliffs, NJ: Prentice Hall.

Aliber, R. Z. (1988) *The International Money Game*, 5th edn, New York: Macmillan.

Buckley, A. (1996) *Multinational Finance*, 3rd edn, London: Prentice Hall.

Eiteman, D. K., Stonehill, A. I. and Moffett, M. H. (1995) *Multinational Business Finance*, 7th edn, Reading, MA: Addison-Wesley.

Eng, M. V., Lees, F. A. and Mauer, L. J. (1995) *Global Finance*, New York: Harper Collins.

Holland, J. B. (1993) *International Financial Management*, 2nd edn, Oxford: Basil Blackwell.

Levi, M. D. (1990) *International Finance: The Markets and Financial Management of Multinational Business*, 2nd edn, New York: McGraw-Hill.

Madura, J. C. (1995). *International Financial Management*, 4th edn, St Paul, MN: West Publishing Co.

Shapiro, A. C. (1992) *Multinational Financial Management*, 4th edn, Needham Heights, MA: Allyn and Bacon.

Stern, J. M. and Chew, D. H. Jr (eds) (1988) *New Developments in International Finance*, Oxford: Basil Blackwell.

Index